REINVENTING THE WHEELS

REINVENTING THE WHEELS

Ford's Spectacular Comeback

Alton F. Doody and Ron Bingaman

BALLINGER PUBLISHING COMPANY
Cambridge, Massachusetts
A Subsidiary of Harper & Row, Publishers, Inc.

International Standard Book Number: 0-88730-330-7

Library of Congress Catalog Card Number: 88-24197

Printed in the United States of America

Library of Congress Cataloging-in-Publication Data

Doody, Alton F.

Reinventing the wheels.

1. Ford Motor Company. 2. Automobile industry and trade—United States. 3. Corporate turnarounds—United States. I. Bingaman, Ron. II. Title.

HD9710.U54F545   1988   338.7'6292'0973   88-24197
ISBN 0-88730-330-7

Contents

Acknowledgments

A book such as this cannot be written in isolation. The authors owe a great deal of recognition and gratitude to the people who contributed vital information, ideas, technical backup, and moral support during the time it took to complete the manuscript.

Special thanks are due Toshiro Yasumori, director and general manager of marketing and sales for the Mazda Motor Corporation of Japan. From the very beginning, Mr. Yasumori offered personal inspiration as well as useful insights into the competitive realities of the international automotive industry. He also helped pave the way for an earlier version of the book that was published in Japan. This created the somewhat curious circumstance wherein a book written by Americans about the resurgence of a key U.S. automaker was translated into Japanese and distributed in Japan before reaching the American market.

The authors also wish to acknowledge the valuable help of Yoshiaki Yamanaka and Tadashi Ono, both executives of Autorama, Inc., of Japan; and Maseo Kawai, director of domestic representation for the Ford Motor Company, Ltd., of Japan.

The authors enjoyed patient, cheerful cooperation and received a wealth of answers, data, and background material from current Ford executives. Among them is Donald Petersen, who succeeded Philip Caldwell as chairman and chief executive officer at Ford.

Other Ford officials who merit special thanks include David W. Scott, vice president for external affairs; Jerry Sloan, executive director for public affairs; Richard Judy, director for external communications; Lewis Veraldi, vice president, car programs management; Charles Gumushian, Paul Preuss, and Kenneth Brown, all of the public affairs group; and Ray Ablondi and Joel Pitcoff of Ford's North American Automotive Operations (NAAO).

Special thanks go to Philip Caldwell, the retired chairman and chief executive officer of the Ford Motor Company. Mr. Caldwell, who is now senior managing director with Shearson Lehman Hutton, Inc., was a key player in the Ford renaissance that is described in this book. The authors are grateful not only for the priceless background information and viewpoints that he offered but also for his graciousness and his willingness to endure a series of probing interviews.

Another Ford retiree who deserves generous thanks is John Sagan, who was treasurer of the Ford Motor Company during its comeback years. Throughout the course of research on the book, Mr. Sagan was an important source of ideas and referrals.

Still in the retiree category, but carrying a wholly different set of credentials, is Doug Fraser, former president of the United Auto Workers (UAW). Without the cooperation and support of Mr. Fraser, his union colleagues, and Ford's rank-and-file workers, there may well have been no Ford "comeback story" to tell. Mr. Fraser, who is now affiliated with Wayne State University in Detroit, provided the authors with very useful information and opinions about the auto industry in general and the Ford Motor Company in particular.

Other sources of important information and ideas were Helmut Schluender of Lapeer, Michigan, the former owner of a Ford supplier company; Thomas Recht, who was in charge of the Taurus account for J. Walter Thompson; Shingo Ino, deputy general manager of J. Walter Thompson of Japan; Richard Chalfin and Thomas Duggins of Visual Services, Inc., Bloomfield Hills, Michigan; Fred and Rhett Ricart of Ricart Ford, Columbus, Ohio (the largest Ford dealership in the world); Terry Prichard, a Ford dealer in Dallas, Texas; Dr. Ezra T. Vogel, professor at Harvard

University; and Dr. Stephen J. Bass, president of Strategic Information Services, Inc., Columbus, Ohio. We also want to thank James Brian Quinn, Dan Dimancescu, and Penny Paquette for sharing portions of their case study on Team Taurus with us.

The authors deeply appreciate the professional advice and moral support of Carol Franco, publisher, Marjorie Richman, editor, and Cindy Buck, copyeditor, of Ballinger Publishing Company. Finally, a note of thanks goes to Mandy Bingaman of Dayton, Ohio, who assisted with technical research, and Nancy Miller of Columbus, Ohio, who typed the manuscript through numerous revisions, ending with a crash deadline for the final draft.

Introduction — Back to Basics

The following story is about one of the most impressive and inspiring corporate turnarounds in the history of American business. It's the story of how the Ford Motor Company rebounded from virtual extinction in the late 1970s to become the world's most profitable automaker and the undisputed leader in a resurgence of American manufacturing quality and productivity.

The turnaround would take more than five years, require the investment of more than $5 billion, involve a revolution in Ford's corporate culture, and culminate in the longest, most elaborate new-car launch program that Detroit had ever seen.

The rebuilding effort at Ford touched every phase, function, nook, and cranny of the company. But as sweeping as it was in its long-term, corporatewide effects, the effort was ultimately identified with a single product: the Taurus. Ford's development of this car — and its twin, the Mercury Sable — was a watershed in American industrial history and aptly symbolizes what America *can* and *must* do if our economy is to have a viable manufacturing sector in the twenty-first century.

The Taurus and Sable were successful from the very beginning, yielding badly needed profits and recapturing a significant share of the U.S. car market for Ford. In fact, *Car and Driver* selected Taurus as one of the world's ten best cars for all three years of its existence: 1986–87–88. And *Road and Track* named the 1988 Taurus the world's best sedan in its class and price range. The Taurus also enjoys an exceptionally high customer satisfaction rating, which was again confirmed by a 1988 *Motor Trend* survey revealing that 91 percent of Taurus owners would buy another Taurus, and 94 percent would buy another Ford product.

In its first two years, the Taurus became America's best-selling mid-size car. This achievement is all the more remarkable given the higher-than-average repair record of the first-year (1986) Taurus and Sable models. Since the Taurus and Sable were totally new cars — built "from the tires up" — it is not surprising that the company would experience some problems at the outset. But, in keeping with its new standards of quality, Ford took pains to follow up and take whatever corrective steps were necessary to fix defective vehicles and then engineer the problems out of succeeding models, as well as current models that are still coming off the assembly line.

Due to the car's immediate popularity, Ford's Atlanta and Chicago assembly plants were running two 10-hour shifts per day in 1987, producing some 550,000 Taurus and Sable units per year. Also in 1987, for the first time in thirty years, Ford surpassed Chevrolet in the production and sale of cars in the United States. Ford's 1987 domestic sales rose by 4.9 percent, while Chevrolet's sales *dropped* by 12 percent.

The Taurus-Sable program gave a powerful boost to the popularity of the entire lineup of Ford and Lincoln-Mercury products. Overall domestic sales by the Ford Motor Company increased by 25,000 units between July 1986, and July 1987, while General Motors sales *decreased* by more than 569,000 units over the same period. In 1986 *Motor Trend* voted the Taurus "Car of the Year" in the United States and named the Sable runner-up. The following year, *Motor Trend* picked the 1987 Ford Thunderbird as "Car of the Year" — thus giving the Ford Motor Company top honors for two straight years. Meanwhile, the Ford Escort was emerging as the best-selling car of any type in the world for six consecutive years (1982-87), with more than 6.5 million sales in 60 countries. And for the first quarter of 1988, three of the five top-selling auto nameplates in the United States were Ford's. The Taurus was America's best-selling car across all classes and market segments; the Escort was second; and the Tempo was fifth.

Not surprisingly, Ford's success in the marketplace was reflected on its profit-and-loss statements. In 1986 the Ford Motor Company out-earned General Motors for the first time in sixty-two years, posting a profit of $3.29 billion, compared to GM's $2.94 billion. In 1987 Ford reaped the highest profit in the history of the auto industry — $4.62 billion, which was a 41 percent increase over the previous year, a full billion dollars higher than GM's earnings, and three and a half times the earnings of Chrysler. With its momentum still building, Ford set two more worldwide auto industry earnings records in the first two quarters of 1988. For the first three months of the year, the company recorded the largest single-quarter profit in history — $1.623 billion, which was $533 million higher than GM and nearly nine times better than Chrysler. The very next quarter — April through June — Ford did it again, topping its own record with earnings of more than $1.66 billion, compared to GM's $1.5 billion and Chrysler's $320 million. At this point, industry analysts were predicting that the company's earnings for all of 1988 would set still another full-year record for the industry.

Ford's success certainly didn't happen overnight. In 1979 the company faced extraordinary circumstances that called for extraordinary measures. Old walls had to be knocked down, professional jealousies quelled, and fiefdoms broken up. Anyone and everyone who could help bring a winning new product to market had to be organized into a cohesive team with a single, unified purpose. Ford had to assemble key people from many different disciplines — from product planning, marketing research, design engineering, production engineering, manufacturing, procurement, logistics, finance, sales and marketing, public relations, personnel, labor relations, legal affairs, advertising, dealer relations, and any other staff specialties that could make a contribution. Ford also realized that it had to go to the factory floor and involve line workers in the development process, and it had to go outside the company to two other groups that historically had been overlooked or short-changed, but who have always had a vital interest in the car business: the suppliers and the customers.

All this might seem quite obvious — almost too sensible to merit any special notice. But for Detroit it was a radical departure. *Nobody* in the cradle of carmaking had ever set out to plan, produce, and bring a new car to market in such a systematic, team-oriented manner. And faced with the desperate need for cost retrenchment and plant modernization, against the backdrop of a struggling national economy, Ford's strategy was anything but predictable, and its purpose anything but routine: to create a truly *new* American car. The Taurus would stand in a class by itself, would rival the best European and Japanese cars, and would rewrite the standards for American automotive quality.

To carry out so ambitious a program, what Ford needed right away was something to bring people together and create a companywide focus of purpose. According to Philip Caldwell, Ford's chairman and CEO through most of the Taurus development years, "It was important that we adopt a few basic principles — not too many for people to deal with all at once — and then demonstrate the dedication and tenacity to see those principles through."

The first such principle was simply to build better products. "Our quality had gotten pretty bad," Caldwell admitted. "But quality is really a *state of mind*. We had to break out of the rut of thinking poor quality and focus our minds — our whole ethic — on *good* quality. Of course, it wouldn't happen merely by thinking about it, but we had to firmly plant the goal in our heads to start with and then refuse to compromise."

The second principle was to concentrate on people. "Most people truly *want* to do the right thing," said Caldwell. "But you have to deal with them straight-up. Be honest and candid with them. We resolved not to try to sugar-coat our problems or play games with our people. We concentrated more on treating our workers and their union representatives as mature adults and as our peers."

Out of these two basic principles — a dedication to product quality and a concentration on the values and dignity of people — arose all of the other operating principles, policies, and methods that produced the Taurus and restored Ford to a competitive posture.

It all sounds almost too simple to be true, or too simplistic as a "management science" methodology. Corporate America is a complex environment in which many people have become too accustomed to seeking only complex solutions. But as Philip Caldwell says, "It's time for American business leaders to get back to the basics."

REINVENTING THE WHEELS

1

Doldrums in Detroit

The foreign-car invasion of the U.S. market had begun inauspiciously enough. From the early 1950s, a small minority of wealthier American motorists and dedicated car buffs had been buying European-made luxury sedans and sports cars. But through the first half of the century and well into the fifties, grassroots Americans hardly knew that cars were manufactured anywhere outside of Detroit. The automobile was viewed as an American original — an exclusive Yankee invention. More than that, it had become virtually a national totem. In the psyches of many American men and even of a few women in those preliberation days — the car, not the home, was a person's "castle." And considering the grandiose scale and style of most Detroit cars through the late 1970s, this analogy was quite fitting.

If, however, the American car was not necessarily viewed by all drivers as a "castle," it was still revered as something far surpassing a mere means of transportation. As noted by historians and social commentators, Americans have long had a love affair with the automobile, sometimes treating it as though it were a living thing: a companion, mistress, lover, best friend, child, or pet. Henry Ford's Model T, for example, inspired outright adoration from a generation of Americans, including not only the "common man," for whom the car was designed, but also celebrities, intellectuals, artists, and writers such as Gertrude Stein, Sinclair Lewis, and E. B. White.

Whether it was viewed as a castle-on-wheels or was given a lifelike personal identity, the American car, in any case, reflected important things about its owner. It both revealed and helped to create social status; it broadcast the owner's individual taste and style; and for many drivers it offered the pleasures of escapism and a chance to fantasize about themselves and their relationships toward the world they lived in.

When the first sprinkling of foreign economy cars began hitting U.S. shores, very few Americans — and least of all the automotive pros in Detroit — believed they would make even a ripple in the mainstream of the nation's car business. The earliest import of note was the Volkswagen Beetle, which was introduced in the United States in 1950 with the sale of 300 cars. The Beetle was considered an odd-looking aberration, a bad imitation of a "real" car, or of what most Americans had been conditioned to think a real car should be. Early Beetle buyers often found themselves the butts of jokes, or worse, the objects of scorn. They supposedly either couldn't afford a real car or were simply social heretics — blasphemers in a nation of car worshipers.

America's Big Three automakers surveyed public opinion on the Beetle and other small imports and concluded that Detroit had no reason to worry. The little aliens might nibble a bit at the *used*-car market, but they would never get a real piece of the pie. Detroit was cocksurely secure in its belief that American drivers would continue to want bigger, plusher, flashier, more powerful cars. A 1952 report from the Ford Division of the Ford Motor Company boasted that, "to the average American, our present car and its size represent an outward symbol of prestige and well-being." In other words, the *real* Mr. and Mrs. America needed a big, showy car to authenticate their self-esteem and keep their neighbors mindful of just how successful and important they were. Only eccentrics and people who lacked patriotic zeal would consent to be seen in an undersized, underdressed, underpowered import.

These notions, and the carmaking strategies they supported, continued to gain credence in Detroit even as the omens gathered and the concrete evidence emerged to reveal their shortsightedness. In 1956, when Volkswagen in particular was starting to make clear inroads into the U.S. market, a high-ranking Ford officer, Ernest Breech, proclaimed that American automakers produced more cars in a single day than Volkswagen sold in an entire year. If he was speaking of Volkswagen sales only in the United States, Breech's assessment may have been statistically defensible at the time he made it. But inside of just two years, it became a hollow, meaningless boast as Volkswagen doubled its North American sales in 1957 and doubled them again in 1958, reaching a total of 104,000 cars in the latter year. Volkswagen, indeed, had come a very long way in a fairly short time. In 1953 Americans had bought only 2,500 Beetles. Thus, during the five-year period from 1953 to 1958, the little German "toys" — as some Americans liked to call them — increased in sales approximately forty-one times over.

Ernest Breech's sweeping comment was symptomatic of the myopia that afflicted Detroit in the 1950s and would continue to blur the vision of U.S. auto executives for nearly three more decades. In fairness to Detroit's decisionmakers, however, it must be noted that the mid-fifties was a remarkably prosperous, heady time in the United States. The nationwide consumption spree that started in the wake of World War II had escalated with the end of the Korean hostilities in 1953. Americans were buying and buying and buying; and one product they were buying in great numbers was the automobile. In 1955, for the first time ever, the U.S. auto industry passed the 7 million-car sales mark for a single year. That year Detroit sold just over 7.4 million autos, shattering the previous record of 6.3 million set in 1950.

Understandably, Detroit figured that it must be doing things right. What did it matter that American cars were gas-guzzlers? Gas was cheap, and there seemed to be no end to the world's oil reserves. And did it matter that Detroit products broke down or rusted out in three or four years? Everyone knew that the name of the game was "planned obsolescence," and the American driver by this time was well conditioned to playing the game. As early as 1923 — still in the adolescence of the auto industry — Alfred P. Sloan, president of General Motors, admitted that a primary reason for changing auto styles every year was to create "a certain amount of dissatisfaction" with older models. (A notable exception to this philosophy was Henry Fold's Model T, which was legendary for its ruggedness, economy, and reliability. It was built to *last* and its styling wasn't changed every year.)

Although the 1950s was a good time to be in the auto business in the United States, there were, of course, a few headaches. Detroit management, for example, had to contend with one of the world's strongest labor unions — the United Auto Workers; and from the immediate post-World War II period on into the 1970s, the UAW, like many other American unions, pressed aggressively for higher wages and more union control over the workplace. In the decades after World War II, the United States also stumbled through several recessionary periods that caused temporary downturns in auto sales. And, as always, the domestic auto manufacturers were vying intensely with one another to expand or protect their individual shares of the market. The total U.S. car market, however, was perceived by Detroit as a captive one. It belonged to a handful of domestic companies, and foreign interlopers simply were not taken seriously.

American automakers were blithely confident that only Detroit was capable of giving American drivers the cars they wanted. But, ironically, in a nation that "wrote the book" on behavioral research and public opinion polling, U.S. car manufacturers didn't *really* know their customers. Detroit was known for spending huge sums on market research, but that didn't mean the top decisionmakers paid much attention to the results. With little or no competition from abroad, and with an increasingly concentrated oligopoly at home, they cavalierly built the cars that *they* wanted to build, and then, in the best tradition of American car selling, they "pushed" the vehicles on customers who usually had no choice but to buy them.

Over the years, Detroit had also failed to develop much ability to project or interpret economic and demographic trends; neither was it noted for dealing intelligently with organized labor, or for staying abreast of advancing technology, which could have contributed to higher quality cars and increased productivity. True, it might have been an American — the first Henry Ford — who pioneered mass production, invented the assembly line, put the nation behind the wheel, and scored one of the world's earliest and greatest consumer hits with his Model T. But Henry Ford's legacy was encrusted in rust by the time the Germans and Japanese came peddling their peculiar-looking little cars.

As the 1950s drew to a close, more foreign-made cars were to be seen on America's roads and streets. In 1958 Americans bought 379,000 imports, and in 1959 they bought 614,000. The reaction of U.S. automakers to these rising figures was to believe simply that, aside from a relatively few eccentrics, some ordinary American drivers were buying foreign cars because they were low-priced. Hardly anyone — except the people who were buying and driving them — seemed to realize, or was willing to admit, that cars like the Beetle and Sweden's Volvo were basically better built and longer lasting than American cars. The imports may not have offered extravagant styling, abundant interior space, creature comforts, or fast acceleration and high speeds; but they were carefully engineered and generally made of higher quality materials. They held the road better, their steering was tighter and more responsive, they didn't rattle, they didn't rust out as fast, and they got much better gas mileage. It was undoubtedly true that many American buyers were first attracted — and continued to be attracted — by the lower price of the imports. But as more people drove them, the imports gained a reputation for *quality* as much as for economy. While Detroit continued to roll out throwaways that rattled, rusted, and steered as though their front ends were made of whipped cream, a gradually increasing number of U.S. drivers bought imports because they *liked* them, not simply because they could afford nothing else.

Sidestepping the quality distinction, many flag-waving detractors argued that small foreign cars were unsafe — that they lacked the power to get out of the path of highballing tractor-trailer rigs, and that they would be pulverized in any run-in with a Cadillac or a Lincoln. But import drivers countered that their cars' better handling characteristics enabled them to avoid collisions that would be unavoidable in a bigger American car with slower, less certain reactions. And a few foreign companies, especially Mercedes-Benz and Volvo, were pioneering the development of smaller and lighter cars that were engineered and built with safety in mind.

Another anti-import argument in those early days was that replacement parts and skilled repair service were expensive and hard to find. But foreign-car owners replied simply that their cars didn't break down nearly as often as American cars, and hence, parts and repairs were not that much of a concern. In any case, parts and service availability was to become a nonissue in only a few years as import dealer networks were established and specialty repair shops began popping up nationwide to service America's growing fleet of imports.

With the U.S. market becoming more receptive to foreign cars, it was inevitable that a few lemons would find their way into the country. The early Fiats from Italy are one example. The very name "Fiat" was sarcastically translated as an acronym for "Fix it again, Tony." To people who had learned to respect the quality of European cars, the Fiat was an embarrassing disappointment; and in fact, the entire line eventually was withdrawn from the United States for a number of years. The Renault Dauphine from France was hardly any better. A rear-engine car, like the VW Beetle, the Dauphine sold well in the United States until buyers became increasingly disillusioned by the lack of parts and generally poor service offered by Renault's weak dealer network.

Even among the higher priced imports, quality was not always what it was made out to be. The Jaguar, in particular, became notorious for its lack of dependability. The car seemed to spend more time in the repair shop than it did on the road. Among the wealthier drivers who owned Jaguars, the standing joke was, "I had to buy *two* of them — one to drive while the other's in the shop."

The earliest Japanese cars to reach the U.S. market were also notable flops. The first Toyota, in 1958, was so inferior that the Japanese quickly pulled it off the market and didn't reintroduce it until they were sure it was thoroughly debugged. Likewise, the first imported Datsun, manufactured by Nissan of Japan, was a dismal failure. First marketed on the West Coast, the Datsun lacked the engine power and braking reliability needed to get safely on and off California's high-speed expressways. Furthermore, it had an inadequate battery and ignition system, which made it hard to start in chilly weather, and it wasn't nearly as rattle-free or rust-resistant as the better made European cars of that period.

It didn't take Toyota and Nissan very long, however, to redeem themselves in the American market. By the mid-1960s, Toyota had returned with a much improved lineup of compacts, and Nissan had begun to earn Americans' respect for its small Datsun pickup truck. Like other Japanese vehicles of that era, the Datsun truck looked comical to most Americans, but it was tough, durable, trouble-free, and economical.

The willingness and quickness of the Japanese to recognize and correct their product flaws, along with their doggedness in pursuing the American market, *might* have been noted more keenly in Detroit and interpreted as harbingers of trouble — but they weren't. U.S. automakers had reacted to the more successful European imports, such as the Volkswagen, by turning out cars that, even if smaller and cheaper than usual, were still products of Detroit's big-car mentality. Motor City executives continued to believe that the compact economy car was a temporary aberration — that mid-twentieth-century Americans, faddish in their behavior, were simply toying with a passing diversion and would sooner than later insist on driving "real" cars again. Trapped by such thinking, Detroit squandered precious years — strategically crucial years — halfheartedly throwing a few stop-gap compacts on the market in answer to a fundamental market change that it didn't understand and didn't want to believe in anyway.

General Motors, for example, responded in part with the Chevrolet Corvair, a car that was either daringly innovative for the Detroit of the early 1960s or a clumsy attempt at one-upping Volkswagen, depending on how one chose to view it. GM's designers put the engine in the rear — the first time such a thing had been done with a modern American production car. But they failed to design a rear-end suspension system that would accommodate the engine's weight and positioning, and Corvair drivers had a perilous time trying to control the car on curves and sharp turns. After a couple of model years, GM corrected the problem, but the early Corvair was a good example of Detroit's rather off-handed, quick-fix response to the import invasion.

In 1957 the American Motors Corporation had also offered its version of a compact economy car: the Rambler. First-year Rambler sales exceeded 100,000, and second-year sales doubled to more than 200,000. But the Rambler was never to become a serious or long-lived challenger to the better imports, or even to its domestic competitors. Like the other early compacts that were hustled off Detroit's drawing boards, it was basically flawed in concept, purpose, and quality. It was underpowered, flimsily built, and basically boring in style.

The Ford Motor Company, meanwhile, brought out the Ford Falcon in 1959. The Falcon was a small, simple, utilitarian car that was conceived and ramrodded through Ford by Robert S. McNamara, who was later to become secretary of defense in the John F. Kennedy administration. McNamara had been one of a group of young executives called the "whiz kids" who were brought to Ford from the Pentagon following World War II. A personally stolid, strait-laced man, McNamara was pretty much of an anomaly in Detroit. What he wanted was a car that was uncomplicated, unpretentious, and economical — and that's what he got with the Falcon. In its first year the Falcon registered sales of just over 417,000, and its early signs of success temporarily reassured many of Detroit's apologists. McNamara's little car appeared to be a suitable alternative to those from abroad.

The Falcon, however, was not especially profitable to the Ford Motor Company. As an economy car, it sold for a low price that left room for only a modest dollar margin of profit. Like the other U.S. automakers, Ford had relied for years on the robust profit margins in its big cars and on the even healthier margins in the various options that big-car buyers were enticed into adding. The Falcon simply didn't deliver on the same scale. And in spite of its being relatively economical and trouble-free for its owners, the Falcon still didn't offer the engineering integrity and quality of workmanship and materials that were becoming standard in European cars.

Entering the 1960s, Detroit was unaware that its fundamental premises of carmaking were being challenged. Even the Edsel debacle — which cost Ford well over $250 million in 1957 and could have been viewed as a public repudiation of Detroit excess — was written off as an isolated misadventure. After all, not every new model brought out by Detroit carried an absolute guarantee of success. There had been individual disappointments and failures before, and there would be others in the future. But U.S. automakers would have been well advised to consider the Edsel disaster from a broader perspective. Big, clumsy, ugly, and inefficient, the Edsel was a consummation of Detroit's philosophy and taste. It was, perversely, the "ultimate" American car; nevertheless, it illustrated Detroit's growing alienation from the American car-buying public. The Edsel's failure was not merely the failure of an individual car — nor even of the Ford Motor Company by itself. GM, Chrysler, and American Motors could just as easily have bred Edsels of their own.

The overlooked message in the Edsel story was that American drivers would put up with only so much before they finally rebelled. The car was bad enough in and of itself, but its failure in the marketplace also reflected an incipient attitude change among American car buyers. An increasing number of U.S. drivers were less inclined to docilely accept whatever Detroit gave them, especially since they were being exposed to new and demonstrably better standards of automotive quality — standards that didn't originate in Detroit.

Of course, GM and the other U.S. automakers were delighted it was Ford that had bombed so badly. Their executives, line workers, and undoubtedly even their janitors got many a belly laugh out of the Edsel. But even though Ford was the company with a corporate headquarters building called the "Glass House," the other Detroit carmakers were not in a very good position to be throwing stones. Where the Edsel went, there but for a handful of exceptional cars went most of Detroit's fleet of ponderous, gaudy, gas-swilling showboats. Bigness and brashness were still the touchstones of American automaking. In the Detroit mentality of that period — as in former times and for years yet to come — "small and economical" meant "puny and cheap." With this view of the imports, Detroit reluctantly, almost disdainfully, built small cars only as a temporary defense against the invasion of the imports. And if not by calculated intent, then perhaps by subliminal motivation, Detroit built *inferior* small cars, thereby reinforcing the myth that small cars were inherently bad. But American consumers were not to remain gullible forever. The all-round quality of most small European cars became unarguable as more and more people drove them and compared them to Detroit's alternatives, both big and small.

Detroit was still to enjoy some very good times in the 1960s, although the decade did start out on a low note for U.S. automakers. In the recession-dampened economy of 1961, retail sales of American-made cars slumped to 5.5 million, down from the previous year's 6.1 million. Over this same period, imports also dropped, from 500,000 to 380,000. The downswing was short-lived, however, as domestic auto sales rebounded dramatically in 1962 to 6.7 million, and imports faded only slightly to 340,000.

By the mid-1960s, the U.S. auto industry appeared to be truly on a roll again. Indeed, it had entered the most robust, prosperous period in its history — a period that would continue into the early 1970s, before the first of the worldwide oil crises bared the cracks in Detroit's foundation. Domestic car sales in 1965 totaled almost 8.8 million, which was an all-time record, eclipsing the previous year's record of 7.6 million. Import sales, meanwhile, had inched up gradually to 570,000 — only slightly better than five years earlier. If it hadn't been for Germany's trusty little VW Beetle, the imports would have caused barely a ripple at that time.

(In 1963 Americans bought 307,000 Beetles, and in 1966 they bought 420,000.)

Detroit bristled with confidence. The U.S. automakers' stumbling, grudging ventures with compact cars in the late 1950s seemed now to be merely an unpleasant memory that they were anxious to forget. Many Detroit executives felt vindicated in their gut-level antagonism toward the small car. It seemed they had proven their point with American drivers — that little cars were intrinsically bad. And while it was obvious that a handful of Americans would continue to buy small foreign cars, the vast majority of U.S. drivers appeared to be dedicated, after all, to Detroit's big-brash-and-boxy product. Detroit happily responded with an outpouring of its traditional big cars, and during the sixties and early seventies, it also gradually made even its "compacts" larger and heavier.

But while Detroit was prospering and perhaps indulging in a bit of self-righteousness, automakers in Europe and Japan were quietly going about the business of designing even higher quality and more fuel-efficient cars. In particular, the Japanese were steadily — almost stealthily, it seemed — upgrading the quality and performance of their exports to a world-class standard of excellence. Following the early entrants — Toyota and Datsun — there was soon to be Mazda, which distinguished itself by featuring the first commercially viable rotary engine. And then there was that brash little company that arose amid the ruins of World War II, first making bicycles, then motorcycles, and finally cars — all under the name of the company's founder, Soichiro Honda.

As foreign carmakers forged ahead in product quality, they also kept their sights set clearly on the American driver. It would still take a few years yet to get Detroit's full attention, but even before the full effects of the first Middle East oil crisis had been felt, better built imports had gradually and almost imperceptibly expanded their share of the U.S. market. From a nominal 4.8 percent share in 1962, the imports slowly rose to an 11.7 percent share in 1969. Along the way, major milestones for the imports were passed — in 1966, when the number of foreign cars sold in the United States reached a record total of 651,000, and in 1968, when it passed the one-million mark (1,031,000).

In Detroit during that period, a few people were beginning to recognize that this slow incursion was actually taking place, but hardly anyone seemed to grasp its real significance. The American automakers' response once again was to throw a collection of hastily conceived "small" cars on the market, and with only a few exceptions, these cars were no better than the first wave that had been offered at the end of the 1950s. Of course, this isn't to say that *all* small American cars were losers. Ford's 1964 Mustang was a legendary success, selling more than 418,000 units in its first year and capturing the imagination of American drivers in a way that few U.S. cars had done for a long while. But the Mustang, while smaller than the typical Detroit product, was a specialty car, with sportiness as its biggest selling point. Cadillac's original Eldorado — a relatively small four-passenger sedan — likewise struck a chord with sophisticated buyers who were able to discriminate between quality and size.

In 1968, with foreign-made cars capturing 10.7 percent of the U.S. market, General Motors imported one of its own cars into the country — the Opel, manufactured by GM in West Germany. The Opel was marketed through Buick dealers, however, and GM had neglected to impress upon them that it actually intended for the car to be *sold*. On the whole, the dealers were disinterested in the car. They didn't take the trouble to learn much about it and taught their salespeople even less about it. In fact, most of them considered it competitive with their Buicks — an attitude with little foundation because the Opel was neither designed nor priced to masquerade as a Buick. Nonetheless, many dealers felt that for every Opel they sold, it meant one less Buick sale.

In 1969 Ford's reaction to the now recognizably relentless advance of the foreign invaders was to bring out the Maverick, a not very distinguished car that still sold 150,000 units in its first six months on the market. The Maverick's initial success might have signaled to Ford and other Detroiters that Americans *wanted* to buy small, economical, domestically made cars, if only the U.S. carmakers would give them something of real quality. But the message still didn't take, and while Detroit vacillated, growing numbers of U.S. drivers turned again to the imports to get what they really wanted.

In 1970 the imports' share of the U.S. market leaped by three and a half percentage points to 15.2 percent. In that year GM offered its Vega, starting out on a high road by spending millions on marketing research, presumably to make certain that the product was right for its target market. Many more millions were spent on a new and highly automated manufacturing facility in Lordstown, Ohio. But these efforts went for naught because GM didn't have a coherent total program worked out. The Vega was basically just one more quick response to the "import problem." Even the creation of the new and expensive Lordstown facility backfired on GM because the company failed to consider the human factors — the mind-set and work ethic of the people who would be on the assembly line. A series of heated confrontations took place at the Lordstown plant between management and the UAW over work practices and job classifications. The core of the issue, ironically, was the very thing that GM had made such a big investment in: the new automated equipment and processes. The result was a shoddy product — a product that would haunt GM for some time and would prove to be a precursor for a long series of poorly made and unimaginative cars in all price ranges.

At about the same time — in 1970 — Ford brought out its Pinto, a subcompact that sold over 250,000 units in its first twelve months. The Pinto, however, was ultimately to bring the Ford Motor Company almost as much grief as the Edsel had. The car's gas tank and the filler neck to the tank could rupture in a collision and fill the inside of the car with gasoline vapor. The tiniest spark would then cause an explosion and fire, and if people were trapped inside, they were virtually doomed. Eventually, Ford was named in more than 100 lawsuits arising from Pinto accidents in which there had been explosions or fires. Between fifty and sixty people were believed to have died, and numerous others were seriously burned in such accidents. Ford maintained that the Pinto's gas tank design and positioning were no more hazardous than those of most other small cars. But regardless of the merits of that argument, the company was forced to bear the onus of having built what consumer advocates and many media people considered to be a death trap. In the minds of a growing number of consumers, the Pinto thus became one more example of the U.S. auto industry's slipshod efforts to hold off its foreign competition.

An event that occurred halfway around the world in mid-1967 had created the backdrop for even more grievous times in Detroit. In June 1967, Israeli and Arab armies fought the so-called Six-Day War, which ended with Israel occupying large chunks of Egyptian, Jordanian, and Syrian territory. A little more than six years later, in October 1973, Egyptian and Syrian forces attacked Israel during the Yom Kippur holy days. Once again, the Israelis defeated the Arab forces, but this time the Middle East oil-producing nations reacted more forcefully to Israel's victory — they embargoed petroleum exports to the West, suddenly thrusting the United States into a monumental fuel crisis.

The United States still had huge underground oil reserves of its own, but Middle Eastern oil had been so cheap that American companies had come to rely upon it instead of investing appreciably in further domestic exploration, drilling, and development. When the flow of Middle Eastern oil was abruptly cut off, the United States was left virtually high and dry. Gasoline prices at the tank suddenly doubled — provided that a tank with gas in it could be found. Service stations throughout the country were swamped with long lines of cars and irritable drivers, and many stations simply had to shut down for lack of supply. The embargo lasted only five months, but it was long enough to convince millions of Americans that a car's fuel efficiency was a very serious matter.

Detroit, with its meager lineup of mediocre compacts, was woefully unprepared for both the 1973 oil crisis and the next few years, during which fuel-efficient imports would steadily fatten their share of the U.S. auto market. In 1973, the year of the Yom Kippur War, imports had a 15.3 percent share of the market. The following year, they inched up to 15.8 percent, but in 1975 they leaped to 18.2 percent. American drivers were clearly getting the message, even if Detroit was not. If you could have a car that was greatly superior to an American car — and at a competitive price — then why drive an overstyled hulk just to keep an

American autoworker on the job at $20 an hour or more? Many import-buyers didn't earn as much themselves as a U.S. autoworker did, and people were getting cynical about the supposed patriotism of shelling out their own limited funds to help subsidize a bloated, wasteful, out-of-touch industry.

But there was still to be some vacillation on the part of the driving public. By 1976, the shock of the oil embargo had worn off. Gasoline was once again plentiful, and while its price at the tank would never again drop as low as 30 cents a gallon, the U.S. government adopted policies that helped keep the price artificially depressed. As a result, there was a temporary swing back to Detroit's beloved big cars, and in 1976 the imports' market share slumped to 14.8 percent. But that was as low as it would ever go. In 1977, imports topped the 2-million-car sales mark for the first time in the U.S. market (2,072,000), and import market share climbed to a new high of 18.5 percent. In 1978 there was a nominal drop-off to 17.7 percent, but from that point on, the curve went steadily upward.

It is certainly inadequate and inaccurate to interpret the success of the imports solely — or even primarily — in terms of oil supplies and gasoline prices. But one more fuel crisis was to add impetus to the imports. From mid 1978 to mid 1979, the Organization of Petroleum Exporting Countries (OPEC) raised oil prices by more than 50 percent, and in December 1979 — at the start of the winter heating season, when energy demand would begin to soar — five OPEC members again boosted prices by over 13 percent. These price increases reflected OPEC's ongoing campaign to expand its control over the world's oil markets. It also reflected, in part, a new and more virulent anti-American attitude in some of the nine predominantly Moslem nations belonging to OPEC. In January 1979, Iran — one of OPEC's biggest producers — had fallen into the hands of the radical Shiite Moslem leader, the Ayatollah Ruhollah Khomeini, who launched a fanatical anti-Western campaign that threatened to engulf the Middle East and once again cut the United States off from a vital source of oil. With the cost of petroleum skyrocketing, and with future supplies in doubt, Americans began avidly snapping up small, fuel-efficient foreign cars again. The imports' market share in 1979 broke 20 percent for the first time ever, ending up at 21.8 percent. In 1980 their share rocketed by almost five percentage points up to 26.7 percent; and by 1986 they commanded 28.3 percent of the U.S. market.

It should be noted here that while total imports from all foreign sources were biting off ever bigger chunks of the American market, the Japanese were advancing their share faster than anyone. In 1974 Japan had just 6.7 percent of the U.S. market, compared to 9.1 percent for all other foreign sources. By 1986, however, the Japanese commanded 20.7 percent, versus just 7.6 percent for everyone else. That was more than a threefold increase in twelve years.

As we have seen, through most of the 1960s and into the first few years of the 1970s, Detroit had been riding high. Auto plants ran at full capacity, auto executives played their internal power games, and nobody worried about a few minicars from Germany, Italy, or Japan. The United Auto Workers also shared in Detroit's prosperity, winning higher wages, more liberal benefits, and cushier work rules.

But the axe was about to fall, and if it hadn't been propelled by the 1973 and 1979 oil crises, it would have fallen sooner or later anyway. Americans, it seemed, were slowly but inexorably learning to appreciate quality — quality of design, of taste, of performance, of safety, and, indeed, quality of economy. Americans were gaining an appreciation for different styles and tastes in everything from clothing to food to wine to automobiles. Changing economics and social standards also meant more two-earner families, and with more two-earner families came more two-*car* families. Perhaps the family car was a big Detroit sedan or station wagon, but the second car might just as well be a small, fun-to-drive, easy-to-maintain vehicle that got twenty-five, thirty, or even thirty-five miles to the gallon.

By 1980, Detroit was in big trouble, and top auto executives had finally begun to realize that the trouble wasn't all a matter of Middle East politics or an underdeveloped domestic oil industry. Even a quick solution to the most recent oil crisis wouldn't reverse the twelve-year-long assault that foreign cars had been making on the U.S. market. The simple fact was that foreign car-makers had made steady and *real* progress in the design and manufacturing of cars. Japanese cars, for example, were no longer merely economical; they were also attractively designed, trouble-free, and easy and fun to drive. They offered amenities and comforts to drivers and passengers, including a surprising amount of interior space for cars that looked so little from the outside.

As the U.S. auto industry grew more desperate, the voices of trade protectionists also grew louder, both in Detroit and in Washington. From 1979 onward, even louder demands were made for imposing quotas or restrictive tariffs on Japanese cars, until eventually the Japanese agreed, with understandable reluctance, to impose ceilings voluntarily on their auto exports to the United States. Ultimately, however, this didn't do much to solve Detroit's problem. As Japanese cars became scarcer and thus higher priced, many Americans simply shifted their attention to other imports. They bought more Volvos, VWs, BMWs, Audis, and Peugeots.

By early 1982, it appeared that Detroit might go the way of the American shoe and steel industries. The country was in a recession, and the Rust Belt of the Northeast and Midwest was in a downright depression. More than a quarter-million American autoworkers were laid off, and that number didn't account for the ripple effect of layoffs in auto-related industries such as rubber, glass, steel, and other car components. To make matters worse, interest rates were astronomical, and people were putting off the purchase of big-ticket items such as cars, for which they had to borrow money at rates that approached 20 percent. Instead, they were patching up their old cars and trying to get a few more years and a few more thousand miles out of them.

The Ford Motor Company was already in a shambles; in 1978 it had recalled more cars than it had produced. Chrysler, too, was struggling to survive, and the American Motors Corporation was little more than a bit player. Only the giant General Motors seemed likely to be a long-term survivor and keep the U.S. automotive industry alive. But the overall numbers continued to get worse. For all of 1982, Americans bought just 5,759,000

U.S.-built cars — the first time in *twenty years* that domestic auto sales had dropped below six million. That same year, import sales in the United States totaled 2,223,000 — a record market share of 27.9 percent up to that time.

Yes, Detroit was in the doldrums. And nothing could be done overnight to dispel the gloom. But as we'll see in the following chapters, Ford was the first to make some of the thoroughgoing changes that Detroit so desperately needed. Bringing about those changes would require money, imagination, courage, and new attitudes. But there was to be nothing especially complex about the process. The Ford Motor Company was about to rediscover and learn to apply a few old-fashioned American fundamentals. And the changes that came would not only rejuvenate Ford but also stir the rest of Detroit from its lethargy. Before long, General Motors and Chrysler would have more than the Japanese and Europeans to worry about. And over the next few years, the Japanese and Europeans would find themselves facing a much tougher competitor in the world's richest automotive market — the United States.

2

Ford Bets
the Company

Many readers will undoubtedly remember an advertising slogan that the Ford Motor Company used for a number of years: "Is there a Ford in your future?"

Most Americans didn't realize it, but during the three-year period of 1980-82 it was touch-and-go as to whether there would be a Ford in *any*body's future. The proud Ford Motor Company, descendant of the man generally credited with founding the U.S. automotive industry, had been America's second most powerful manufacturing organization in the mid-to-late 1970s. But by the start of the 1980s, it was on the verge of total collapse. In 1978 Ford stock had averaged $32 on the Dow Jones index, but in 1981 it dropped to an average of only $16. For three straight years the company suffered enormous net losses: $1.54 billion in 1980, $1.06 billion in 1981, and $658 million in 1982 — a total loss of nearly $3.26 billion in three years. Meanwhile, factory sales of Ford cars in the U.S. had plunged from 2.63 million vehicles in 1978 to 1.27 million in 1982.

Part of this sales decline was due to a recession-induced slump that afflicted the entire U.S. auto market, but Ford's market share was also taking a beating from General Motors and from Japanese and European imports. The reason was threefold: (1) the tremendous financial strength of GM permitted it to outpromote and outsell Ford, even with products that were not demonstrably better; (2) the quality and price-value benefits of the imports were gaining wider acceptance among American drivers; and (3) Ford's own domestic product quality had been steadily slipping. The Ford share of the American passenger-car market plummeted from 23.6 percent in 1978 to 16.6 percent in 1981. That was nearly a one-third loss of share in three years.

If it hadn't been for the company's own overseas operations, especially in Europe, Ford quite possibly would have gone bankrupt. In 1979 approximately 38 percent of all the Ford cars and trucks sold worldwide were sold outside of North America. In 1980 that figure rose to 44 percent, and in 1981 it was 45 percent. In other words, about four of every ten Ford vehicles sold from 1979 to 1981 were sold overseas. This was nothing new, because Ford had been beating all other U.S. manufacturers in foreign sales for quite some time. In fact, 1981 was the seventeenth consecutive year in which Ford sold more vehicles abroad than any other American automotive company. And from 1980 to 1981, while the company was losing heavily on the home front, Ford's share of the worldwide vehicle market rose from 12.2 percent to 12.6 percent. General Motors might have been far and away the dominant power in the domestic market, but the Ford nameplate was America's number-one entry almost everywhere else.

This was one of the important legacies left by the original Henry Ford and cultivated further by Henry Ford II. From its very beginning, the company had been more internationally inclined than most U.S. industrial firms. As early as August 1903, just two months after the Ford Motor Company was founded, the first Model A was sold in Canada, and over the next few years Ford plants were built in Britain, France, and elsewhere. The company was operating in Europe and even in Argentina as far back as

1905 and 1906. World Wars I and II, of course, derailed the company's European operations, but both disruptions proved only temporary. Following World War II and the post-war reconstruction of the European economies, Henry Ford II led the company in a rebuilding program which, by the 1970s, made it one of the biggest, most prosperous industrial organizations of *any* type in that part of the world.

Ford was and is the biggest auto company operating multinationally in Europe. West Germany had its Volkswagen, Audi, Mercedes-Benz, and BMW; Italy its Fiat; Britain its BMC; and Sweden its Volvo — but Ford's operations spanned the whole non-Communist European community and produced cars that outsold many of the European and all of the American nameplates in large segments of that community. The company also operated in virtually all other parts of the non-Communist world — in some 175 countries and territories altogether — but Ford of Europe had long been the most profitable arm of the overseas organization. During the shaky period of 1980-82, it was the backbone that kept the whole corporation from going prostrate. There was a curious twist to this situation: in order to succeed in Europe, Ford had to build cars that Europeans would drive — cars that by the 1960s and 1970s were generally smaller, better engineered, simpler in style, and considerably more economical than their Detroit cousins. What was good for Europe, it appeared, was not good for America — at least not yet.

The circumstances were not without their irony. The U.S. auto industry — Ford included — blamed "unfair" foreign competition for the catastrophic state in which it found itself at the start of the 1980s. In fact, Ford's was among the loudest voices demanding federal legislation to restrict imports. Yet here was the company of old Henry Ford, one of the earliest multinational industrial leaders, both blaming foreigners for its problems and depending heavily upon foreigners for its very existence.

The changing makeup of Ford's work force during this period also reflected the company's dependence upon foreign operations and sales. In 1978 somewhat more than half of the company's workers worldwide were employed in the United States, but by

1981 that proportion had dropped to considerably below half. Over the three-year period, the average number of employees worldwide fell from 512,000 to 411,000 — a decline of about 101,000 jobs — *85,000* of which came off the U.S. payroll.

But the Ford Motor Company could not be sustained indefinitely by its foreign operations alone. Its fixed investment back home was simply too big, and it was losing too much money on its domestic operations. Most Ford vehicles sold overseas were also manufactured overseas under more favorable cost structures; thus, they could be priced competitively and still yield a reasonable profit. But the company's foreign successes bore little relationship to what was happening in the home market — except to pump badly needed money in at the corporate level to keep ailing domestic operations afloat. And in 1979 domestic operations were quite sick from a number of maladies: sharply declining sales and loss of market share; high labor costs and anemic productivity; deteriorating plants and archaic machinery; a lineup of mediocre products; a loss of consumer confidence; and a lack of any exciting or promising new-product ideas on the drawing boards.

Ford's close brush with extinction in the early 1980s was partly obscured from public knowledge because of the similar life-and-death struggle at Chrysler, which got all the headlines and television airtime. Lee Iacocca, the former Ford president who took over the failing Chrysler corporation in 1979, waged a media campaign and applied his charismatic sales and political skills in persuading Congress and the Federal Reserve Board to help rescue the company. Playing heavily on the impact of foreign competition, Iacocca turned Chrysler's plight into an "us-or-them" patriotic issue and talked the government into a $1.2 billion loan guarantee for what would become known as the "Chrysler bailout."

Without this benign federal intervention, America's Big Three automakers would have become the Big Two, leaving only General Motors and Ford clinging to a vastly diminished U.S. share of the worldwide automotive market — a share that, in spite of Ford's continuing overseas success, had eroded from more than 76 percent in 1950 to less than 21 percent in 1980. The one other formerly sizable U.S. automaker at the start of the 1980s — the American Motors Corporation — had slipped to only a nominal presence in the industry by this time.

As the drama swirled around Lee Iacocca and the Chrysler bailout, the situation at Ford grew more grim. The company's working capital plunged alarmingly from $2.3 billion in 1979 to less than $237 million in 1981 — a ten-fold drop in just two years. At the time, in fact, some industry observers felt that the government was rescuing the wrong company. A collapse of the much larger Ford organization would have been a far heavier blow to the U.S. economy and would have opened the gates even wider to the imports. Furthermore, it would have seriously diminished America's most significant presence in overseas automotive markets.

At stake, too, was the historic, institutional importance of Ford, not only to the U.S. economy but to the nation's cultural heritage and self-image as well. Ford might have become "worldly" because of its long-time foreign successes, but the company nonetheless was — and is — "apple-pie American." Even though it was ruled quite imperiously by the original Henry Ford and rather autocratically by his grandson Henry Ford II, the company had always projected a grass-roots American image. It was, after all, the company that had produced the Model T — the world's first "car for the masses." And in spite of some ugly labor conflicts in the 1920s and 1930s, Ford had generally maintained the aura of a "workingman's" company. With the exception of its Lincoln luxury cars, Ford products have typically been middle-class, shirtsleeve American.

The liquidation of an institution such as Ford would not only have been a crippling loss to U.S. industry but also a poignant disappointment to many ordinary citizens. Yet, in 1981 this was a very real prospect. Although Ford was not literally at the brink of bankruptcy, as was Chrysler, the company nonetheless was in deep trouble. If something hadn't been done quickly to revitalize its domestic automotive operations, Ford might have ceased to be, in a real sense, an American carmaker. The company could very well have been forced into mergers with foreign automakers in order to protect its vast worldwide investments, while preserving only the remnants of a corporate identity.

In June 1980, *Fortune* magazine had speculated that Ford had "no more than four years to turn its North American divisions around or face illiquidity." Three months later, *Time* magazine declared that Ford was "in many ways even sicker than Chrysler."

By mid-winter of 1980-81, Ford's predicament, though still largely unappreciated by the general public, was arousing increasing concern in the business press and financial circles. In February 1981, *Business Week* reported that Ford's financial condition was "rapidly deteriorating." The magazine predicted that the company would have a hard time generating the billions of dollars it would take to maintain a serious presence in the American auto market. And in April 1981, *Newsweek* and the *Los Angeles Times* spoke in terms of imminent doom. *Newsweek* warned that Ford had "no room left for mistakes," and the L.A. *Times* stated flatly, "The giant Ford is now on its knees." After three-quarters of a century, the company that had put America's middle class on wheels was running on paper-thin treads itself.

Or so it seemed. But the Ford Motor Company had always displayed a particular strength: *resiliency*. Over the years, Ford had weathered other crises and had bounced back from other failures. During the heavy-handed tenure of the first Henry Ford, there had been brutal and costly struggles with organized labor. There had also been the Edsel, as well as the Pinto's exploding gas tanks. Yet the company always seemed to have something in reserve: if not, like General Motors, a hoard of cash, then a new idea — or a fresh face with new ideas.

Henry Ford II was the last member of the Ford family to truly dominate the company. He had taken command in September 1945, just weeks after the surrender of Japan ended World War II. Perhaps there is some poetic irony in the timing of his reign. He took charge of the firm almost simultaneously with the crushing defeat of Japan, but when he retired thirty-four years later in 1979, he relinquished the reins of a company which by then was almost mortally wounded — in part, because of the peace-time resurgence of the Japanese.

Certainly, it wasn't Japanese imports alone that had brought the younger Henry's company to the brink. But he and his compatriot American auto magnates, as well as union leaders, autoworkers, and politicians, tended to credit — or malign — the Japanese for much of the domestic industry's troubles. In any case, the departure of Henry II from the Ford throne meant the passing of an old — and tired — regime at the nation's number-two car company. And without meaning to denigrate Henry II's leadership or accomplishments, one might say that his departure was none too soon. The Ford Motor Company, like the rest of the Detroit establishment, needed a whole new set of attitudes and values. If Ford was to survive — and with it, ultimately, the entire U.S. auto industry — the old premises of carmaking had to be junked. Detroit's cars themselves were throwaways; so, too, were Detroit's carmaking ideas and standards.

When Henry Ford II retired in October 1979, he was succeeded by Philip Caldwell, a twenty-six year Ford veteran who was thoroughly schooled in the old ways of making cars — the Ford ways and the Detroit ways. Thus, there was no sudden infusion of new blood into the corporate body. In fact, Philip Caldwell had been groomed for and steered into the top job by Henry II himself.

Much has been written about the internal power struggle at Ford during the middle and late 1970s, when Lee Iacocca was maneuvering for the chairmanship and CEO's office. Iacocca had been Ford's president since December 1970, and many people — including Lee Iacocca — had good reason to view him as the logical successor to Henry Ford II. However, Henry II had developed an intense personal dislike for Iacocca, and as the decade of the seventies neared its end, some of Ford's presumed successes under the Iacocca presidency were increasingly seen as having been more illusion than fact. Meanwhile, Philip Caldwell had been steadily and quietly building up a set of credentials that would weigh in his favor when Henry II eventually stepped down.

In March 1977, Henry Ford had told Caldwell, "I want *you* to succeed me." A month later, Henry created a new three-man Office of the Chief Executive, with himself remaining as chairman, and Iacocca as president, but with a totally new position of "vice chairman" for Caldwell. This triumvirate was to stay in place until Henry could resolve the dilemma of Lee Iacocca. During that time, Caldwell would be engaged at the highest level of decisionmaking in the company and would be at least a peer, if not a superior, to Lee Iacocca.

Shortly after the Office of the Chief Executive was created, Henry II planned his own retirement for approximately three years later — or late 1980. This three-year timetable was shortened by a year, however, as the result of two events. In July 1978, Henry II fired Iacocca, thus clearing Caldwell's path to the top. Then, in the summer of 1979, Henry II became ill with a heart problem. Not wishing to leave his succession up for grabs in the event of his death or incapacitation, he named Caldwell president in October 1979. For all practical purposes, Caldwell at that point was running the company, even though Henry Ford held onto the title of chairman for several more months. Finally, in March 1980, he told Caldwell, "It's ridiculous for me to stay on as chairman. Since you're the one who's running the company, you ought to have the title." Thus, Caldwell became chairman and chief executive officer, while another Ford veteran, Donald Petersen, was moved up to president and chief operating officer.

For several years prior to Lee Iacocca's firing, a determined faction inside the company believed that Iacocca was the ideal choice for the top job, and eventually perhaps a third or more of the outside directors held the same view. Many industry observers with no actual connection to the company had also been exposed to Iacocca's magnetic personality, and more than a few of them presumed that he would become the first person from outside the Ford family to head the corporation. Even after Philip Caldwell had become vice chairman, and thus shared the "chief executive's" role with Henry Ford and Iacocca, there were people who found it hard to believe that Iacocca would be by-passed in favor of Caldwell. Iacocca was the consummate salesman — the type of catalyst that many people felt the company desperately needed.

Caldwell's leadership capabilities were questioned in some circles, primarily because of his low-key personality, which contrasted so sharply with Iacocca's flamboyance and charisma. Some felt that Caldwell was too much a product of the entrenched Ford system — a system which, presumably, Iacocca would re-enliven and stir to dramatic action. Others thought of Caldwell as somewhat stodgy, indecisive, and too cautious to be a strong, inspiring leader. But a sufficient number of high-ranking executives, board members, and influential outsiders considered Caldwell to be exactly what Ford needed — perhaps partly *because* of those very qualities that distinguished him so much from Iacocca: his methodical, deliberate, *un*spectacular approach to management. He was known as a systematic person who not only could see the "big picture" but also believed in tending to the details. John Sagan, retired Ford treasurer who served during the company's turnaround years, describes Caldwell as "thoughtful, compassionate, oriented to long-range thinking, and less opportunistic than Lee Iacocca."

No one could deny that the Ford Motor Company at that time was out of control and that it had to be brought back to the basics. It had to become leaner, better attuned to the current realities of the marketplace, and more proactive than reactive. Caldwell's temperament and background seemed, on balance, to make him ideally qualified for the tough and unglamorous job of setting priorities, sculpting solid plans, and trimming the fat from the company. He would, indeed, bring a new perspective to Ford, but it would not come in a bright flash of inspiration. It would emerge gradually as the result of hundreds of day-by-day, incremental decisions and changes.

Caldwell was already an experienced "turnaround" manager. In 1970 Henry Ford II had sent him to Ford's Philco Division — a radio and appliance manufacturer that was in a sorry mess — and Caldwell had turned it into a profitable operation that Ford was later able to sell for a good price. The job he did with Philco did not involve any especially unusual or innovative measures, but was simply a matter of down-to-basics, hard-nosed management.

Caldwell's solution was to shut down aging and unproductive factories — many of which were only half full — slash costs everywhere possible, streamline production methods, and bring manufacturing capacity into a better balance with the sales levels that Philco could realistically expect to sustain. It was also significant — and a somewhat novel idea in American industry at that time — that he emphasized improved product *quality*.

Having dealt successfully with Philco, Caldwell returned to his preferred line of trade, the automotive business, where he was to remain for the rest of his tenure with Ford.

While solidly versed in the American way of making cars and trucks, Philip Caldwell enjoyed the extra advantage of knowing how the Europeans did it. In 1972 Henry Ford II sent him to Europe, where he headed up Ford of Europe for approximately a year. Caldwell was then brought back to Detroit, where he managed all of Ford's international automotive operations until 1977. During this period, however, he retained special "oversight" responsibilities for Ford of Europe, and his continued exposure to European design, engineering, and production standards couldn't help but influence his product philosophy, as well as his technical know-how.

From the very beginning of the auto age, the European view of the car was quite different from the American view. Through the first half of the century, Americans, with vast supplies of cheap domestic petroleum, could afford to drive heavy, boxy vehicles that got only eight, ten, or twelve miles per gallon; but European cars had to be fuel-efficient because most of Europe had little or no oil. Until the North Sea oil fields were developed in the mid-seventies, most of western and northern Europe had to import the bulk of its oil from the Middle East and other parts of the world, and to discourage extravagant use of petroleum, governments imposed heavy taxes on automotive fuel. Gasoline was not only more expensive but its availability for private automotive use was often less certain. For a long while after the birth of the automobile, most European countries, in fact, tried to prevent their economies from becoming oil-dependent. European industry for many years ran primarily on coal, a resource that was plentiful both on the Continent and in the British Isles. Thus, automotive fuel was a premium commodity in Europe, and that geoeconomic fact contributed to Europeans and Americans embracing totally different concepts of what a car should be and how it should perform.

A car's fuel efficiency depends partly upon the design and engineering of its motor, carburetion system, and complete drivetrain, but it also depends upon the vehicle's overall size, weight, and the aerodynamics of its body style. In the interest of fuel efficiency, European cars typically have been smaller and lighter weight than American cars, and, while not all of them have offered the best possible aerodynamics, they have tended to be more streamlined and less cluttered with exterior gingerbread. The size limitation on European cars also mandated more efficient — and less luxurious — treatment of interior space: hence the "austereness" of the typical European production car.

The need for fuel efficiency certainly hasn't been the sole reason for the "European look." Social attitudes and tastes — in addition to general economic conditions — have also been important determinants. Through most of the twentieth century, Europe simply hasn't enjoyed the level of prosperity that America has. Europeans couldn't afford to be as wasteful. They've had to build cars and many other products that would last longer and function more economically. All of these factors help explain why Ford had built different kinds of vehicles for its domestic and European markets.

Philip Caldwell wasn't the first — nor would he be the last — American auto executive to be exposed to European influences; and in any case, it would be both an exaggeration and an oversimplification to suggest that he merely copied European standards and methods of carmaking. Furthermore, by the late seventies, the Japanese were reshaping the global auto industry. And while Ford had never had as much presence in Japan as it had in Europe, the company was beginning to look to the Japanese both for ideas and for opportunities. Ford had bought 25 percent of the Mazda Motor Corporation at the suggestion of a Japanese bank that controlled Mazda. The bank asked for Ford's help after the first version of Mazda's rotary engine proved so poor in fuel efficiency and durability that it nearly bankrupted the company. American auto firms had been kept out of Japan since before World War II — although there were times when Ford and others had dealerships there. Thus, the invitation to buy into Mazda gave Ford a golden opportunity to reestablish a presence in Japan, and despite its misadventure with the first rotary engine, Mazda was still an important player in the car business.

Regardless of Ford's European and Japanese connections, when Caldwell moved into the top job, he inherited a lineup of vehicles that were generally overweight, dully styled, gas-hungry, breakdown-prone, and notorious for rusting out in short order. Product quality at Ford had become an embarrassing subject, and Caldwell resolved to bring that subject out of the closet and to make it a priority issue companywide. First, however, he had to take some drastic actions to ensure the company's immediate survival.

Since fixed costs represent a huge proportion of the overall costs of auto manufacturing, making deep and permanent cutbacks was unavoidable. One of Caldwell's first painful steps in this direction was to slash 250,000 cars out of scheduled production for mid-year 1980. This, of course, was a short-term move that hardly began to make a dent in fixed costs; but it was a start. If that many fewer cars were to be built — cars that weren't selling anyway — then payroll could be trimmed to help stem some of the immediate hemorrhaging of cash. In 1980 Ford's average hourly labor cost (wages and benefits) was $19.99 — roughly comparable to GM's, and somewhat higher than Chrysler's.

Altogether, the Ford Motor Company reduced its corporatewide domestic work force by nearly 60,000 employees from 1979 through 1980 and by almost 9,000 in the following year. Cuts in the workforce were by no means concentrated among hourly production workers, but included thousands of salaried staff and executive personnel. Ford, in fact, has continued to trim its salaried staff even after leveling off cutbacks in hourly production jobs. From 1979 through 1987, the company has reduced what it calls its "ongoing automotive-related salaried positions" by 36 percent worldwide — or by a total of 44,000 jobs. During the early retrenchment in 1979-80, Ford also pared down executive salaries and perks. In addition, five unproductive plants were ticketed for shutdown, and within the next four years, two more plants were closed. Over an eighteen-month period spanning 1980 and 1981, Caldwell and his management team purged approximately $2.5 billion from fixed costs, and in the following year they lopped off another $500 million. Ford's weight-loss program was well under way, and the company was to become leaner yet.

Explaining the cost-reduction campaign, Caldwell said: "We had to think the unthinkable and achieve the seemingly impossible. It took a major effort to generate economies of the scale that was necessary. It required looking at the entire organization and seeing what could be changed, slimmed down, or dispensed with. It meant doing a lot of things we would much rather have avoided, because human beings were involved. But we had to do it to survive."

A new company advertising slogan — "Quality is job one" — would come to symbolize one of Ford's most dramatic departures from the Detroit norm. In 1978, prior to a meeting of senior management, Caldwell was privately jotting down a checklist of discussion priorities, and at the top of the list he wrote, "quality — number one." Out of this casual beginning arose a distinct new product philosophy. The term *job one* is carmaking jargon for the first car of a new model as it starts down the assembly line. By declaring "Quality is job one," Ford was saying that quality would be the first "component" to go into every new car and that it would accompany the car all the way down the line. Caldwell carried the concept even further when he said, "The quality I am talking about is not limited to products or to our manufacturing and assembly plants. Quality is an ethic, a course of action to govern everything we do."

This objective might seem simple enough, logical enough, and as honorable as motherhood and the flag. But for several decades, the concept of quality had inspired little more than lip service in Detroit. The difference now was that Philip Caldwell really *meant* it. What's more, it was an absolute imperative. Growing numbers of Americans were switching to foreign-made cars, no longer so much because of price, or even for the sake of fuel efficiency, but increasingly and decidedly because of superior *overall* quality. Quality was more, too, than merely a perception in the minds of import-buyers. The superior quality of foreign cars was a tangible, measurable trait. Hertz Rent-a-Car kept detailed maintenance and repair records on its auto fleet, and in 1979 those records revealed that Japanese cars were *twice* as well made as American cars. It was almost incredible, but no longer deniable, that a "Made in the U.S.A." label now connoted what "Made in Japan" had meant to most people in the 1950s — shabbily made, tasteless, and inferior.

In Detroit the quality gap was a hard reality to face, and closing that gap was to be no easy job — even if you did make it job one. The task was difficult for many reasons, not the least of which was a need to define the very meaning of quality as it applied to a car. At the top of Detroit's quality checklist for years were priorities such as a high-horsepower engine, a fluffy ride, a big body, a plush interior, and lots of chrome. But too many Americans were foregoing those presumed marks of excellence in favor of something else that still seemed to escape Detroit's understanding. European carmakers had lived by this "something else" for more than half a century, and the Japanese had caught onto it and mastered it in only a dozen years or so. Now, in 1979, Detroit had to figure it out — and there was precious little time in which to do it.

It wasn't really such a fathomless mystery. The answer was there to see if Detroit, for a change, would just look outward instead of inward. To define quality and identify the standards by which quality could be judged, American carmakers had to consult American drivers. And they had to *listen*, as they had never listened before, to what the nation's drivers were saying. It was long past time — if ever, indeed, there had been a good time — for presuming that the masterminds of Detroit knew unerringly what was best for the American car buyer. Sizable numbers of American car buyers had already voted against

Detroit's version of quality; they had voted with the dollars they spent for superior foreign cars.

Automotive quality cannot be measured in terms of the individual components that go into a car, such as pistons, gears, struts, or stereo speakers. Neither is quality necessarily reflected in a car's aesthetics or styling (although in 1980 many people in Detroit still seemed to think so). It's important, of course, that components be made of high-grade, dependable, durable materials — good steel, for example, or good safety glass for the windows. But one of the key reasons why Europe and Japan had outdistanced Detroit in overall quality was because their executives and designers viewed a car as a *totality* — as a complex but unified system of interrelated functions and features all working together to give the driver and passenger a pleasing experience. Their cars were conceived and constructed to *fit the driver and passengers*, while most Detroit cars were built to satisfy the technical and aesthetic prejudices of their makers.

Philip Caldwell had already committed Ford to the ambitious goal of catching up to and eventually surpassing the quality of Japanese and European cars. Ford, he decreed, would become both a domestic and world leader in automotive styling, safety, engineering, construction, and durability. It would build the best cars to come out of Detroit in many years, and in doing that, Ford would not only regain its financial health but also help regenerate pride in American workmanship.

That, of course, was a very tall order. It involved, first of all, adopting the driver/passenger design focus that had been absent for so long from Detroit's way of thinking, and this would mean a painful uprooting of deeply embedded ideas about design, engineering, ride, production methods, and even promotion and marketing techniques. It also meant painstaking research and an exhaustive, objective analysis of Ford's weaknesses and the competition's strengths. It required a new and less adversarial relationship with labor and dramatic improvements in employee motivation. It would involve making some gutsy, risky decisions. And it would cost a great deal of money, because many of Ford's production facilities were outmoded. New high-tech machines —

including robotics and electronic process controls — were needed to ensure precision and to upgrade efficiency and productivity.

Eventually, all of these changes would require an enormous investment. Considering the company's deteriorating financial and market position, it would amount to "betting the company" — that is, laying the company's very existence on the line for a single, all-out effort. As will become evident in the following chapters, however, Ford's "bet" was an extraordinarily *calculated* risk — not, as Philip Caldwell is quick to point out, "a roll of the dice or a spin of the roulette wheel."

Caldwell wasn't in any sense the whole story behind the coming renaissance at Ford. Certainly, as chairman and chief executive officer he charted the course and enunciated the new goals. Quality would be the top priority; excess plant capacity would be eliminated; advanced technology would be adopted; productivity would be raised; distinctive new products would be developed; and Ford's image would be restored to respectability in the home market. But one of the most important principles underpinning the entire effort was the idea of *teamwork*. Under Caldwell's stewardship, there were no longer to be any heroes at Ford. No autocrats. No blazing stars. No swashbuckling personalities, with their attendant cults and cliques. This philosophy was a drastic break from Detroit tradition, because the American auto industry had almost always been a stage upon which single-minded, egocentric, and sometimes tyrannical men had played out medievalesque intrigues and frequently brutal executive war games. There had been more superstars than supercars in Detroit's history. Now, however, the number-one man at the number-two company said it was time to take off the greasepaint and get down to serious business — a business that was languishing under the star system and could survive now only through teamwork, cooperation, and the input of all the diverse talents that could be mustered.

Among the key talents at Ford during this period were Donald E. Petersen and Harold A. ("Red") Poling. Petersen, with twenty-five years of experience at Ford, had been named president and chief operating officer when Henry Ford II elevated

Philip Caldwell to the chairmanship. He was basically a product-oriented man, known to automotive writers as a "car guy." Poling, an experienced finance man, had been given the tough job of carrying out Philip Caldwell's no-nonsense cost-cutting program. Over the next five years, these two men were to collaborate with Caldwell in orchestrating a venture that was unique to the American car business.

Something drastic had to be done to set Ford products apart from the rest of the Detroit pack, and it wasn't enough merely to reshape the shells around existing platforms and drivetrains or to spruce up a few details and add a few customer come-on features.

"We committed ourselves to the design, manufacture, and sale of superb products, with no excuses," said Caldwell. "They were to be *drivers'* cars — functional, comfortable, good-looking, and distinctive."

What Caldwell really wanted was a car created from scratch and built upon a rationale all its own. "We took a new approach in function and appearance," he said. "We had to have the courage to be different, but not in frivolous or superficial ways."

As important as function and value-for-money, then, was the need for a boldly different style. When Caldwell first started talking about radically new styling, however, his intentions were viewed by many at Ford with skepticism. Designers had heard such talk before, but in the end, senior management and the finance department had always backed away from anything that was truly innovative. In the past, it had been deemed safer to stick with the familiar, especially if what was familiar had the ring of the bell-cow of the U.S. industry — General Motors. Certainly, there had been an occasional divergence, but Ford design over the years had essentially echoed the angular, squared-off look of GM's products.

In Ford's Detroit design shop at that time was a man named Jack Telnack, who had been head of design for Ford of Europe in the 1970s. Telnack, like Philip Caldwell, had thus been heavily exposed to the Europeans' soft, rounded, more aerodynamic styling. In fact, he had pioneered this design profile for Ford of Europe during the same period when aerostyling was being adopted by Audi and Mercedes-Benz. Yet when told that Caldwell wanted to establish a new Ford look for the American market, he didn't assume that the chairman might be receptive to anything as drastically different as the aeroshape. Everyone knew that boldness and imagination can sometimes be oxygen-starved in the rarefied air of the boardroom and CEO's office. Telnack was encouraged by the expressed intent to go for a new look, but he and other Ford designers worked cautiously for some time before it became clear to them that top management was dead serious about doing something extraordinary.

The first manifestation of Ford's new aerodynamic look came in February 1983 with the Ford Thunderbird and Mercury Cougar, both of which bore little outward resemblance to their popular predecessors. The smaller Ford Tempo and Mercury Topaz, introduced for the first time in May 1983, were also aero-dynamically styled — as was the Lincoln Continental Mark VII, which was released in the fall of 1983. With the public acceptance of these cars, Ford had finally broken away from the prevailing American design profile, replacing the boxy look with the aeroshape — a shape which some critics and competitors described as the "eggshell look."

When Jack Telnack was working on the design of the 1983 Thunderbird, Donald Petersen urged him to design the kind of car that he himself would want to be seen driving. This was an unheard-of experience for a Detroit production-car designer. At another point, Philip Caldwell also encouraged Telnack to "reach for a really different design." But Philip Caldwell's concept of a totally new and distinctively different Ford automobile had still not been realized. In early 1980 the team was being formed and the guidelines were being laid to produce such a car.

The financial investment in the Taurus-Sable program was, in itself, a historic decision for Ford because it was the largest investment the company had ever made in a single new-product development effort. Shortly after he became chairman, Philip Caldwell asked key staff and line executives what it would cost to create a *totally new* family of cars, starting from raw concept and seeing the products all the way through to the dealers' showrooms. The resulting estimate was $3.1 billion. But that was just for the development of the first models of the new product family: the Taurus for the Ford Division and the Sable for Lincoln-Mercury. In the meantime, money was also needed for modernizing plants and re-engineering better quality into the company's other product lines. After further calculation, Caldwell and his staff added approximately $2 billion to the $3.1 billion needed for the Taurus-Sable program, then took the resulting $5.1 billion figure to the board of directors. This sum actually represented the ante that Ford had to put up at that time to remain in the high-stakes competition with GM and the foreign carmakers. But some of the media seized on $5.1 billion as the cost of developing the Taurus and Sable. Caldwell says this was an oversimplification at best.

"I really don't know why that $5.1 billion figure got so much attention," he says. "It's even oversimplifying things to say that it cost $3.1 billion to create the Taurus and Sable, because you just can't isolate all the costs that neatly. We were dealing at the time with a *total* effort to create better quality products, raise our productivity, and get a bigger share of the market. And we were contending with all the government regulatory demands on fuel efficiency, emission controls, and safety. Whether we're talking about $3.1 billion or $5.1 billion, it was still only a part of what was going to be a much larger ongoing investment. And let's not forget, either, that we had already invested a lot of money to meet the new government regulations. Back in the mid-seventies, when Washington started laying really heavy demands on the industry, a group of economists got together and estimated what it would cost for the whole domestic industry to do everything that was being mandated. They figured it would take $40 billion for GM, $20 billion for Ford, and another $20 billion for the rest of the companies, including key suppliers."

The $5.1 billion that Ford committed in 1980 might be thought of as part of the company's "share" in bringing the whole U.S. industry up to speed. But Caldwell makes it clear that the people at Ford never considered the Taurus-Sable program, or any of the other improvements, to be their share of an industrywide burden. Their mission was focused on only one kind of "share" — a bigger share of the American car market for the Ford Motor Company.

In any case, the $5.1 billion commitment was an enormous investment for a company that was already staggered by heavy losses and facing an uncertain future in a tremulous economy. The commitment, in fact, represented *half* of the company's net worth at that time, and not all of Ford's board members were eager to vote for it. But Ford had no truly competitive cars in the markets that counted. Eventually, Caldwell, Don Petersen, and other key executives were able to enlist enough support to get the program approved. As Caldwell explained later, "There really wasn't any choice. The only alternative was to get out of the car business altogether and get into something else."

While Ford chose to put all this money into the development of a new product, General Motors, by contrast, was investing heavily in new technology and new plants, rather than new cars. General Motors, of course, didn't lack for the resources to do both things simultaneously — and in a big way. But the two companies' strategic leadership was different. Ford, with comparatively limited financial resources, elected to go straight into the battle of the marketplace; GM opted to spend the time and money building impressive new plants and stockpiling new high-tech weaponry. By the late 1980s, Ford's decision is looking better all the time.

3

Taurus — A Bright
New Constellation

S ome called it a "jellybean," a "flying potato" — and worse.
Some said it was merely a copy of Germany's aero-
dynamically styled Audi 5000. Others predicted it would never
win the hearts of citizens in America's heartland. But Ford was
to have its new car, the distinctively different car — the *unique*
car — that Philip Caldwell had hoped for.

Caldwell himself had retired from Ford's chairmanship and
had vacated the CEO's office by the time the car went on the
streets. But it was he who had issued the mandate, shaped the
extraordinary organization, and cultivated the unconventional
mind-set that had all coalesced in five and a half years to produce the car he believed Americans wanted and needed.

It was the Taurus. And it was, in the opinion of most
qualified automotive observers as well as that of many ordinary
car buyers, the freshest, most imaginative and carefully thought-
out product to emerge from Detroit in practically anyone's
memory. No American car had ever been conceived as purpose-
fully, planned as painstakingly, or produced as intelligently and
efficiently.

Detroit had always birthed its new cars the natural way: first, a gleam in somebody's eye; then a burst of passion; and finally, a long period of waiting, intense labor pains, and a messy delivery. Nobody ever really knew what was going to pop out until it was actually there, squawling, sometimes misshapen, and in need of a good cleaning up.

One problem was that Detroit was incestuous. True, the U.S. automakers competed aggressively with one another in the marketplace, but their products and their methods of doing business all sprang from the same family of ideas. More importantly, Detroit carmakers were locked into a static, rote, reactive procedure for creating supposedly new products.

After Philip Caldwell had laid out the objective of building a distinctively new car, Ford might have followed the ordinary pattern of development, and the result would have been, most likely, an undistinguished product — a product that would have done little, if anything, to improve the company's chance of survival. This ordinary, or conventional, process of development was what Ford executives came to describe as "sequential." It consisted of a series of unrelated, uncoordinated activities carried out by people who were insulated from one another in their own narrowly defined areas of specialization. The unwritten and heretofore unchallenged rule was that certain things had to be done before others, and that each area of specialization was sacrosanct; no set of experts had any business meddling in other experts' affairs.

The birthing of a new vehicle typically began with the product planners, who generated an overall concept of the vehicle's basic dimensions, style, and equipment content. These product planners, however, did not usually enjoy a great deal of creative freedom. They worked, instead, within the constraints of the often ethereal and sometimes ephemeral vision of a car that top management felt the public ought to have.

From the product planners, the vehicle's development was shunted to the design engineers, who translated the more or less abstract design into concrete form: clay scale models and mock-ups.

Next, the job was passed along to the specifications engineers, whose job was to draw up the nuts-and-bolts requirements that would determine and demonstrate how the artistic creation could actually be turned into a car.

After the various engineers had done their work, the manufacturing specialists were responsible for figuring out how all the components would be built and brought together, and how the car would make its journey down the assembly line. Some of these specialists were internal company people, and others were outside suppliers who were expected to build components according to the specifications of the automaker's engineers.

As the cars rolled off the assembly line, the company's marketing department had the task of selling them (at least those that had passed inspection). Later, when an unpredictable number of the cars broke down, the dealers and sometimes the company's own service specialists had to fix them.

At various times, or in various stages of the car's tortured trek from concept to service bay, there were still other specialized jobs and events going on that would affect the car's ultimate success. Company finance people, for example, had to compute costs and establish budgets for producing and marketing the car, and they had to price the car to suit its intended market and yield the hoped-for profit. The legal department, meanwhile, had to make sure the car met various government regulations concerning safety, fuel efficiency, noise, and pollution controls. Labor relations people were interested in whether or not the car could be built within union work-rule constraints. Procurement and inventory control specialists arranged for the purchase and timely availability of materials. And public relations experts had to prepare the public for the new car and court the attention (preferably favorable) of the automotive press.

The results of this system were poor communications, territorialism, buck-passing, and squandered opportunities. People from different departments or specialties didn't speak the same dialect or share a common purpose. There were professional jealousies, interdepartmental rivalries, and a widespread tendency to blame somebody else for anything that went wrong. If too many cars were coming off the line with defects, the manufacturing specialists, designers, and engineers found it easy to blame one another. If a car didn't sell as well as expected, the marketing people might blame the finance people for pricing it too high, and the finance people might blame just about anybody who came to mind. One Ford executive described the situation in the mid-seventies as civil war.

Predictably, sequential development was reinforced by the functional structure that had evolved at Ford. Donald Petersen once labeled that structure a collection of vertical "chimneys." Each function was a self-contained, vertical unit, and one chimney's managers usually didn't communicate very well with their counterparts in other chimneys. The problems created by a chimney structure, however, were not by any means unique to Ford. It was the Detroit way. Managers at General Motors, Chrysler, and American Motors also marched to their own beat. So, too, had those at many other U.S. auto firms who had already marched with their companies right over the edge into oblivion.

If Ford was to gamble the company on an unknown product, there was an opportunity — even a compelling reason — for starting with a totally new approach. Ford needed somehow to break down its chimneys so that its managers, instead of working vertically and in isolation, could communicate horizontally and work together. Facing such a challenge, Ford might have chosen the costly and disruptive strategy of massive reorganization. Whole new divisions and departments might have been created, and old ones eliminated, with people getting shuffled around like colored pins on a corkboard. And, in the end, the chimneys would have simply been relocated and repopulated with similar mixes of people. But that didn't happen. Instead, Ford's new leadership style ("no more heroes") seems to have been the stimulus behind the dismantling of the chimneys. The result was a new atmosphere that encouraged the creation of coordinated, project-oriented teams of people with diverse talents — teams such as the one that would develop the Taurus.

Development of the Taurus began in late 1979 under the code name "Sigma" and was originally a project of the company's advanced vehicle department. Heading the department at that time was Lewis C. Veraldi, who later became the vice president for car programs management. As the Sigma project evolved and the vision of a new car began to take shape in people's minds, the development team itself continued to grow until, eventually, it numbered several hundred people. Jack Telnack was placed in charge of design. In the spring of 1980, the code name Sigma was dropped, and the team got a new name: "Team Taurus."

In most cases, a great deal of brainstorming and research goes into the naming of a new car. Marketing and advertising people know full well that regardless of how good (or bad) a car is, its name alone can imprint an indelible picture in consumers' minds. There have even been a few horror stories in this connection. The Chevrolet Nova, for example, inspired a less than auspicious reception in Mexico before somebody at General Motors realized that the Spanish term *no va* means "no go." Nissan of Japan also went through some interesting exercises in selecting names for its early exports to the United States. Instead of a Datsun, for example, Americans might have been looking at Japanese cars with names such as Lion, Tiger, Bluebonnet, or Fair Lady, which were among a few of the alternatives proposed by Nissan management. The Ford Motor Company itself had played the name game very seriously over the years. Henry Ford II was quite sensitive about the names of his cars. More than 5,000 suggestions were considered before the Thunderbird got its name. Despite the reluctance of Henry Ford II to name a car after his father, the Edsel got its name largely by default after some 18,000 prospective names were screened and rejected. Ford had even commissioned a New York poet, Marianne Moore, to invent a name for the doomed car, but her suggestions probably wouldn't have saved it anyway. Among her offerings were Resilient Bullet, Mongoose Civique, and Utopian Turtletop.

The Taurus got its name in a much less complicated way. Lewis Veraldi and his planning director, John W. Risk, were talking one day in early 1980 and discovered through casual remarks that their wives shared the astrological sign Taurus. There was nothing deleterious or embarrassingly funny about the name, so they decided it could be used at least as a working appellation for the development team. Later, the company tested the name through consumer research and got very positive reactions. Moreover, the name Taurus seemed appropriate for a product that bore the burden of saving its company. In Greek mythology, Taurus is a cosmic constellation containing the Pleiades, seven stars that represent the seven daughters of Atlas, who was the titan bearing the weight of the world on his shoulders. Astrologically, the Taurus personality is deemed to be faithful, deliberate, determined, and practical — all of which are qualities that one might find desirable in a family car. And in the bigger arena — that is, the American auto industry's fight for survival — the name Taurus suggested the brute power, tenacity, and pride of a bull.

As for the Sable, the connotations of the name are less dramatic but still interesting. A sable is a weasel-like animal that is native to northern Europe and Asia and that yields a sleek, richly toned, blackish-brown fur. Its fur has always been highly prized and reflects an image of tastefulness and class. That's certainly a desirable image for a car that is meant to stand apart from the crowd, and the Mercury Sable is intended to do just that. While virtually identical to the Taurus mechanically, the Sable has a somewhat sleeker, more stylish exterior and a plusher interior. It is also 2.5 inches longer than the Taurus, giving it 1.5 cubic feet more interior space. The two cars are most distinguishable from each other in their front-end design. The Sable has a single, flush, transparent plastic strip running the width of the front and covering the headlights. The Taurus headlights are also covered but are separated by a smooth, metal center band that contains the Ford emblem suspended in such a way as to make it appear to be floating. The net effect of the subtle styling differences is enough to make the Sable appear sportier and a little more dashing: hence its appeal to a target market of younger, style-conscious buyers. The Taurus, on the other hand, looks rather heavier, more substantial, and slightly subdued in style to appeal to young and middle-aged family-oriented buyers.

44

From the spring into the summer of 1980, Team Taurus not only grew in size but also took on greater clarity of purpose, which Lewis Veraldi segmented into four basic parts:

1. The team was to create a *world-class car*, with quality second to none — either domestic or foreign.
2. The *customer* would be the focal point in defining quality.
3. *Product integrity* would never be compromised.
4. To accommodate the first three objectives, the team at the very beginning had to involve people from both *"upstream"* and *"downstream"* in the carmaking process: that is, from the CEO's office to the design studios to the end of the assembly line — and even beyond, to the supplier, the ad agency, the dealership, and ultimately, the customer.

Besides making the first three objectives more attainable, Veraldi's fourth objective had a corollary purpose: to replace *sequential* development with *concurrent* development. For example, soliciting manufacturing's input upstream in the design process would make manufacturing's job easier and better integrated with design objectives when the project later came downstream — through engineering to the factory floor. With all the departments working concurrently rather than sequentially, all the benefits of real teamwork would be more achievable.

It's impossible to overstate the importance of the team aspect of Team Taurus. Of course, the basic idea of teamwork as a good way to get a job done was hardly a novel idea. It has been talked about in business schools, management seminars, and scholarly journals for quite a while. Even in the auto industry, GM had long embraced an official credo that presumably subordinated individuality for the good of the organization.

But in the folklore of the American automobile business, the great legends have typically been woven around *individuals* — not groups or teams. The Motor City and those writing about the Motor City like to talk about their creative geniuses, their "movers and shakers." Bold, colorful, workaholic, domineering personalities stir the emotions and fascinate the imaginations of the less audacious man and woman in the street. They also feed the presses of both the business and popular media. The Henry Fords, Lee Iacoccas, and John DeLoreans — not to mention the Walter Reuthers — have always been "good copy."

At the Ford Motor Company in late 1979 and early 1980, however, the value system that accommodated such individual stardom was on its way out. No Lone Rangers would be riding to the rescue at Ford. The "hero" would be a *product*, not a person, and the success of that product would be attributable to and shared by everybody who had anything to do with it. Eventually, even the office and shop rhetoric would change. From an "I" company, Ford would become a "we" company. People started saying "we," "us," and "our" instead of "I," "me," and "mine."

This change was not merely cosmetic, and it reflected something far more than a new etiquette or protocol. What was really happening at Ford was a transformation of the *corporate culture*. People were actually changing the way they viewed the company and how they interpreted their roles within it. It was certainly not to be an overnight phenomenon, because there are too many subcultures inside and around a giant organization like Ford to permit instantaneous or easy change. Corporate executives and union leaders, for example, have traditionally approached their jobs and dealt with one another from widely differing perspectives and premises. So, too, have engineers and stylists, accountants and manufacturing people, marketers and lawyers. Getting such diverse types of people to listen to one another, respect one another's ideas and problems, and collaborate closely in a team effort is both a delicate and large order.

Between late 1979 and 1986, however, Ford's Team Taurus accomplished just that. It not only created and launched the new product that the company so badly needed, but also was instrumental in creating a new environment within the company — a new corporate culture.

Since Team Taurus was responsible not merely for the development of a new car but literally for the future of the entire corporation, it was imperative that its decisions be based on real knowledge rather than on guesswork, wishful thinking, or flashes of inspiration. As *Newsweek* magazine was to say a year later, Ford had "no room left for mistakes."

One of the first orders of business was to develop a realistic picture of the American car market, both present and future. Ford had to know, with as much reliability as possible, what kind of a car would be most appealing to American drivers five years down the road. For Detroit, this was not an unusual time frame. It had almost always taken American automakers four to five years — from conception to launch — to bring out a new model. This isn't to say, however, that they had always used those years to the best advantage in terms of research. Considering the amount of time traditionally involved, they might have done a better job of reading the market — if not with pinpoint accuracy, then at least with a little better feel for the customer. But as we've discussed earlier, Detroit had rarely allowed customer needs and wants to interfere with the arcane art of carmaking.

With the Taurus program, however, Ford made a different kind of commitment. For the first time ever, the *customer* would come *first*. This meant serious research, right from the beginning and all the way through the development process, to ensure that Team Taurus remained on target. Furthermore, Ford needed to understand more clearly its overall position in the marketplace. Everybody knew things were bad and were likely to get worse, but it wasn't enough simply to blame imports or even to admit that Ford quality was unacceptably low. The company still needed to know what was on consumers' minds. What, specifically, didn't they like about Ford or its products or its dealers? Exactly what did they find so much better about the competition, both domestic and foreign? What would they like to see Ford do — and would they return to the fold if Ford did it? All of these questions, let alone the immediate need to get a competitive new car on the market, called for a totally new philosophy of marketing research. Or, as Donald Petersen said, "Maybe we'd better do it right for a change, and do the research before making the decisions."

Marketing research at Ford had long been a central corporate staff function operating out of World Headquarters at the Glass

House. This lofty position separated the research people from many of the day-to-day operating realities of the company. Bureaucratic snobbery came easily — at the expense of good intra-company communications. Marketing researchers sometimes took advantage of their corporate-level, big-shot mystique to embarrass members of other operating groups. This, quite naturally, bred suspicion and resentment, even when it wasn't warranted. Whether the research group was doing a good job or not, many people still viewed it with distrust. Just as damaging was the fact that the researchers, isolated as they were from the mainstream of product planning, didn't always address the germane issues or pursue the hard questions that needed answering in other operational areas.

With the enormous commitment that had been made to the Taurus program, something as vital as marketing research could not be left hovering above the battle. Petty jealousies, caste-consciousness, and internecine feuding had to be stopped, and the research professionals had to join ranks with everybody else. What's more, everybody else had to accept them in a spirit of cooperation and mutual respect. In 1980 Red Poling, who was then in charge of Ford's North American Automotive Operations (NAAO), persuaded Petersen and Caldwell to reassign a large part of the marketing research staff to his operation. A few researchers remained attached to the worldwide corporate marketing staff, but most were transferred out of the world headquarters environment and placed in the operating unit that was responsible for actually producing and selling cars in the United States.

Louis Ross, head of NAAO's Car Product Development Group, was one of the people who had been urging just such an integration of marketing research into the total team effort. When the change was made, he put the rest of NAAO on notice that the newcomers were to be treated as compatriots and as specialists who had a unique contribution to make to the team.

"If you ask these people to do research," he told his staff, "you'd better listen to them, and if you don't want to follow their research findings, you'd better have a very good reason."

Once marketing research was attached to NAAO, its top priority was Team Taurus, and research personnel became working members of the team. They were no longer oracles who passed along sacred edicts from the dizzying heights of World Headquarters. Working side by side with designers, engineers, manufacturing specialists, finance people, marketers, and other key operating personnel, they could become more sensitive to the complexities of putting an automobile together. Their research, therefore, could be focused more tightly on practical, day-to-day knowledge requirements, and they could present their findings in a less threatening manner than before because they were now insiders. They were *team* members.

The head of the marketing research group that moved to NAAO was Ray Ablondi. Faced with the challenge of organizing and managing a research program unlike any that had ever been undertaken by a U.S. carmaker, Ablondi first developed a master plan. The objective of this plan was to identify the specific, concrete ways in which research could contribute to or reinforce the overall team effort. Research for the sake of research was of no interest. Beyond this quite obvious constraint, the *timing* of research activities was of crucial importance. Ablondi's master plan had to be geared to the specific make-or-break decision points that naturally occur in the continuing development of a new car. There would be moments when final decisions had to be made before development could proceed further, and Ablondi's plan had to be timed to accommodate these known decision points. There would also be "unnatural" — or unforeseen — decision points where such things as changing costs or perhaps new consumer research findings would either dictate a break from the original project plan or require a backtracking and redirection in the car's development. This latter sort of contingency was difficult to prepare for, but if research was well coordinated and time-phased with the basic, normal flow of development, then the whole team would be more resilient and capable of dealing with the unexpected.

Such resiliency did, in fact, come into play more than once during the creation of the Taurus. For example, in April 1981, more than a year after development had begun, the overall size of the car was drastically changed. As Lewis Veraldi put it, "We scrapped the whole car." That was something of an overstatement, because the basic conceptual design and quality standards, among other things, were not scrapped. But the car was reengineered to be bigger than originally intended, and this was done because of a perceived change in the targeted market. When planning had first started on the Taurus project, the national and world economies were still experiencing tremors from the second Mideast-induced oil shock of the late 1970s. Gasoline prices were then expected to keep climbing to as much as $2.00 or even $3.00 a gallon. Fuel efficiency had become an overriding priority, and since a car's size and weight are major determinants of fuel efficiency, the Taurus had started out as a rather small car. In early 1981, however, there were signs that gasoline prices would level off and that by late 1985, when Taurus was scheduled to reach the market, Americans would again prefer larger, more imposing-looking cars. Team Taurus reached a consensus that the car as originally designed would be too small. So it was back to the drawing board — and in all possible haste. The small prototype of Taurus was expanded in all dimensions. Its wheelbase was enlarged, its track was widened, and its overall volume was increased.

Lewis Veraldi was convinced that such a mid-course change in direction could not have been maneuvered under the old methods of development. "Without the simultaneous process of the team approach," said Veraldi, "so much time would have been lost that we probably wouldn't have been able to accomplish all the changes in design. With the team approach, everyone was in on the change. It came as no surprise, and thus could be planned for and adjusted to accordingly. The only time lost was the time it took to make the new, larger prototype — about eight months of non-stop work."

One of the critical discoveries that surfaced early in the Taurus marketing research effort was a surprising new consumer perception of the entire company. Some Ford officials had presumed that the public was angry with the firm. But what they found may have been even more disturbing. Research showed that Americans, especially those on the West Coast, weren't really angry with Ford — they simply didn't care. They were indifferent! It's one thing to be disliked; quite another to be ignored. The patriotic pride and confidence of a great many Americans might have been wounded if a long-standing institution like Ford had actually folded. But meanwhile, Americans were getting the cars they wanted — from other sources.

This discovery led Ford to only one reasonable conclusion: forget about the company mystique, because Ford no longer had one. Forget, too, about patriotism, tradition, or anything else of that sort. In the words of Ray Ablondi, "the only thing that mattered was *customer satisfaction.*" If Ford made the right kind of car available at the right price, convinced people that it really *was* good, and then serviced it properly after it was in the customer's hands, the company would be able to sell more cars. And if Ford kept on doing this, the company name might once again be a household word in America.

The overall marketing research program for Team Taurus was far more extensive and exhaustive than any such program ever conducted by Ford or by any other U.S. auto manufacturer. Researchers interviewed more people than had ever been interviewed before in connection with a single new car model. They covered more territory geographically, taking readings of consumer attitudes in many places outside the usual test-market areas. One example of the intensity of consumer research conducted on the Taurus was an expedition into Marin County, California, just north of San Francisco. In Marin County the research team assembled some 4,500 people in group sessions and conducted consumer tests using fifty Fords, along with thirty European and twenty Japanese cars.

Researchers also asked more questions about specific car features and driver concerns than were typical of Detroit marketing research. In some cases, the team showed Taurus (and Sable) mock-ups to a group of people, went back to those same people and let them drive prototypes of the cars, and then went back to them yet a third time after recommended changes had been made. This procedure was atypical for both Ford and Detroit as a whole. Ordinarily, the company would hold a "product clinic" and invite a small number of consumers to look at either an exterior or interior mock-up of a new car in its early design stage. But those same people would never, or rarely ever, be asked back or given a chance to drive a prototype; they hardly ever even saw the car again until the finished product was on the market. With the Taurus program, however, Ford officials knew they could afford the extra research expense — because they could *not* afford surprises.

The most important focus of consumer research in the early stages was the styling of the Taurus. To begin with, Jack Telnack had finally taken Philip Caldwell and Donald Petersen at their word and had designed a car with a radically new look for Detroit. The soft, ovoid style was so different from the boxy, angular shape of mainstream American cars that many people at Ford were uneasy about how the public would react. It was true that the company was already committing to the production of other models of quite similar shape. The first of these were to be the Thunderbird and Cougar, scheduled for introduction in February 1983. Both of these cars, however, were targeted for markets considerably different from the ones the Taurus and Sable were intended to reach. The Thunderbird and Cougar were ticketed for youthful, sporty, non-conservative buyers — the types of people who are fashion-conscious and who like to think of themselves as being in the vanguard of new styles and trends. The Taurus, on the other hand, was to be Ford's meat-and-potatoes car; as such, it had to appeal not to a narrowly defined and relatively small segment or niche of the market but to a much broader assortment and greater number of buyers.

The Taurus was to be aimed at what Detroit calls the "mid-market," which is concentrated among middle- and upper-middle-income families, a large number of whom tend to be somewhat conservative in taste and oriented more toward utility and economy than toward cutting-edge style. Ford was hoping this market would include many young professional families — the vast number of "baby boomers" — who might otherwise be buying European or Japanese family-size cars. But Ford would be taking a calculated risk in offering this market something that it hoped would be perceived as excitingly new. The danger was that too many mid-market buyers might consider the Taurus styling to be uncomfortably strange, too futuristic, or perhaps even *too* "European."

From a combination of experience, instinct, and preliminary studies, however, Ford researchers already knew how the Taurus styling would be received in one corner of the market — those people who are relatively forward-looking in their thinking and their tastes. Most of these people would approve of the Taurus design and could be identified as upscale buyers, yuppies, car buffs, and "California types."

In automotive marketing research, one of the highly important variables is geography. Regardless of how car buyers may be classified according to income, occupation, age, or other market-segmenting characteristics, many of them also tend to follow a geographical bias in their choice of cars. Size and styling preferences, especially, seem to vary by region or even by state. Certain types of cars, for example, sell better in Texas than in Ohio; New Yorkers buy more of a certain car than Kentuckians; the Deep South has different car tastes than the Rocky Mountain States; and so on.

Probably no car buyer, however, stands out more distinctly from the general population than does the Californian. With its penchant for youth worship, sportiness, and offbeat lifestyles, California is the nation's bellwether for new trends, unconventional ideas, and innovative products of all types. Where automobiles are concerned, a car with a truly different look will often be enthusiastically received in California, while perhaps stirring only mild interest, or failing altogether, in other parts of the country.

Aside from a car's exterior styling and overall panache, one feature that seems to preoccupy a majority of Californians is the "cockpit." California drivers are especially interested in the way the car feels and looks from the driver's seat and are particularly aware of the personal — even intimate — car-driver relationship, which involves the entire "package" of features surrounding and affecting the driver's own space in the car. When Ford researchers showed mock-ups of the Taurus to Californians, the Golden Staters almost invariably spent a great deal of time sitting in the driver's seat and absorbing the aura of the car's cockpit. They were intrigued by the Taurus's drastically new dashboard design, instrument configuration, and other driver-friendly appointments. By contrast, when the car was previewed in Rochester, New York, consumers were more interested in the *back*seat. After a more or less cursory inspection of the cockpit, most upstate New Yorkers opened the rear doors, climbed in, and tried out the rear seat compartment, which would have to be suitable for hauling around tots and teenagers, as well as mothers-in-law.

Geographic distinctions aside, Ford researchers also knew that a certain percentage of the American driving population would adamantly dislike the Taurus styling. These would be the types of people — whether in California, Rochester, or South Carolina — who are almost always unreceptive to anything new or different. Ford designers labeled them "Johnny Lunchbuckets" and, for all practical purposes, these customers were written off as being unreachable — at least for the first model year or two.

Spanning a number of market segments was another group that was difficult to define, but very important in terms of conquest sales. It was called the "twilight market" and consisted of people who vacillate between foreign and domestic cars, or who own both foreign and domestic cars simultaneously. The changeable, equivocal car-buying behavior of these people suggested that they were both quality-conscious and receptive to new and different products. If offered a truly *good* American car, especially one with a totally new look, many of these people would be potential Taurus or Sable customers.

There were undoubtedly many people who initially might be uncomfortable with the car's aesthetics but who, through persuasion and understanding, could be brought to appreciate the practical benefits of its aerodynamic design. And if true love followed, then so much the better. Ford, after all, was more interested in lasting relationships than in fleeting infatuations. The company needed to build, or rebuild, a solid constituency of people who would buy Ford cars out of a sense of confidence and conviction. This would require education — and a two-way sort of education, at that. Ford's research people were already studying car buyers as no automotive researchers had ever studied them; but marketing research would go beyond its customary bounds in ferreting out existing consumer attitudes and preferences. It would actually assist in rationalizing attitudes and in changing preferences. In short, the market was to be educated, briefed, and conditioned to appreciate the Taurus and Sable for what they really were, instead of what they merely seemed to be.

In the accomplishment of this task, Ford actually invoked the ghost of the discredited notion that Detroit knew what was best for the American driver. Before the Taurus finally reached the market, Team Taurus would disregard or override certain consumer likes and dislikes, even when those likes and dislikes were explicitly revealed through marketing research. Far from reflecting the arbitrariness and arrogance of "old" Detroit, however, these decisions were part of a calculated effort to improve the customer's understanding and appreciation of automotive quality, performance, and aesthetics. It should be recalled that Team Taurus's mission was to build the very best mid-market car that anyone could build. This meant creating a rationally conceived, coherent, functioning piece of equipment; it did *not* mean tacking together an assortment of features to satisfy any and all of the perceived wants and whims that might emanate from the marketplace.

It was a matter of protecting the integrity of the product, and it was not by any means a simple task. Design and engineering might call for one thing, but research readings of customer preferences might seem to dictate another. In the end, every such conflict, real or apparent, had to be resolved in terms of the *totality* of the car.

The issue of white sidewall tires presented Team Taurus with one such judgment call. For just about as long as anyone could remember, large and mid-sized American cars had been rolled onto the market on gleaming white sidewalls. It was almost an article of faith. Even though whitewall tires were used nowhere else in the world as original new-car equipment, Americans seemed to consider them an almost indispensable accessory. Until Team Taurus came along, no Detroit automaker would have dared to offer a major new model in the Taurus class without white sidewalls, at least as an option. Members of Team Taurus, however, did not envision white tires as compatible with either the car's styling or the overall image of a world-class car. Europe and Japan had been designing and building quality cars that looked just as good without the affectation of "white spats." And if Taurus was to claim its place among world-class cars, it should be able to do so on the strength of its simplicity and symmetry of design, which white tires would only serve to disrupt visually.

Such decisions, necessary as they were to maintaining the car's unity and clarity of purpose, placed an added burden on the people who would have to promote and sell the car. Public relations, advertising, and sales would have to find new and perhaps subtle ways of explaining, informing, and persuading. They would, indeed, have to educate the market as to why certain things about the Taurus were so different from the norm.

In short, the marketing research role within the team transcended traditional research techniques and parameters. The objective was not merely to "give the lady what she wants," but to tell the lady why she might want to change her viewpoint or consider an alternative.

This new research philosophy contrasted sharply with the approach that General Motors seemed still to be using during this period. GM's 1985 and 1986 Cadillacs, for example, had been brilliantly downsized and restyled with trimmer, cleaner, sleeker lines. But consumer research showed that some customers were beginning to view GM's lineup of Buicks, Oldsmobiles, and Cadillacs as a parade of look-alikes. Many Cadillac owners, especially, seemed dissatisfied with the smaller look of their cars. The new Cadillacs apparently weren't "Caddy" enough for them. GM, perhaps fearing a full-scale revolt by Cadillac traditionalists, hastily responded in a superficial, stop-gap manner. On the 1987 Cadillac, the company extended both the front and rear bumpers by a few inches to make the car look longer and heavier. The change was purely cosmetic. It added or improved nothing in terms of the car's efficiency, driving ease, or safety. In fact, the opposite was the case. The only things added were cost, weight, and bulk; the changes even made the car more difficult to park. Furthermore, the integrity of the car's original design had been compromised. Part of the gracefulness and balance of the car's styling was sacrificed for the sake of allowing a few people to feel they were once again driving a "big" Cadillac.

Undoubtedly, GM's patchwork job on the 1987 Cadillac rescued a certain number of potentially lost sales. But the sapient question is whether the change was in the best *long-run* interests of the company or its customers. Instead of reacting superficially to what was a basically whimsical customer preference, GM might have taken the longer view and tried to educate its Cadillac public to the virtues of the *whole* car — a car that was beautifully balanced and well engineered to begin with. General Motors had invested some $3 billion in developing its new large-car series, which included the 1985-86 Cadillacs. This was identical to the sum that Ford committed to the Taurus-Sable program. Yet unlike Ford, GM seemed rather quick to doubt its own intentions. Given the prevailing attitude at Ford from 1980 onward, it was very unlikely that Ford would have reacted in the same way to what was essentially an isolated consumer complaint.

During the research for this book, the subject of the Cadillac bumpers came up in interviews with Ford officials. The reaction, typically, was a smile and a comment like, "GM is going through the motions, but they're still not *really* listening to the customer."

Behind this response is the key to the new research and development mentality at Ford. Research is no longer a spectator event. You don't merely watch the consumers and hear what they say. They may tell you *anything*. They may say they want or don't want this or that — but are they making informed choices? Detroit had been shoving its pet creations down the consumers' throats for so long that a large number of American car buyers didn't know — and still don't know — how to tell the difference between a good and a bad car. And, to be realistic, one must recognize that most people don't have the time, background, or inclination to be very knowledgeable or discriminating about the many factors and features that go into the making of a car.

It isn't enough, then, merely to listen to what customers are saying, and then go with the flow. The Team Taurus approach was what might be called "creative listening." An effort was made to probe behind consumer responses and to understand why people felt the way they did. The team knew that, in order to put a new world-class car on the American market, it was impossible to satisfy every conceivable consumer preference. The objective was to isolate those planned features that might be least understood in the market. With this kind of knowledge, it would then be feasible to begin educating and changing the opinions of the targeted customers well in advance of the actual release of the new cars.

4

The Four Fs:
Form, Function, Fit, and
Finish

F*orm follows function.* This is designer Jack Telnack's
professional motto (originated by the legendary architect
Frank Lloyd Wright), and it was the key principle behind Ford's
design and engineering of the Taurus.

In the past, most American cars had been developed backwards. Form was considered first. Size, shape, and fashion features
were designed, and then engineers tried to build function *into*
the established styling.

At the start of the Taurus-Sable program, however, Ford said,
"Let's turn this thing around; let's decide first what the new cars
are supposed to *do*, how they're supposed to perform, and then
build the shape around the function."

Of course, the company was also intent upon establishing
its own unique style — its own design profile — to set its cars
apart from GM's, as well as from everyone else's. But the goal
wasn't merely to create a new style for the sake of new styling.

Function would be decided first, and the styling would then be developed to accommodate and complement that function. This process was almost certain to produce a new look anyway, because the overall performance — or totality of function — of the new cars was to be so different from anything else coming out of Detroit.

Certain basic decisions had been formalized early on in the program. For example, it was decided that the cars would have front-wheel drive. That choice, however, hadn't been unanimous from the very beginning. Donald Petersen opposed it at first, while Harold Poling favored it. This was interesting in and of itself. Petersen was the "car man" who presumably would have been partial to the technical benefits of front-wheel drive; but he wondered if, under the company's strained financial circumstances, the enormous cost of engineering and of retrofitting the assembly lines could be justified. Poling, on the other hand, was the finance-oriented man who should have been delighted to save the extra hundreds of millions of dollars. But Poling's reasoning was that front-wheel drive was almost a necessity in light of the continuing uncertainties over oil supplies and gasoline prices. Poling also argued — and consumer research supported his view — that the American public increasingly associated front-wheel drive with advanced automotive technology, and if the Taurus was to be America's most innovative new car, many consumers might be skeptical if it didn't have this feature. In the end, according to Philip Caldwell, marketing advantage out-weighed cost in the decision to adopt front-wheel drive. "We weren't really eager to spend the money," he says, "but front-wheel drive was too important a marketing factor, especially for an all-new car."

Another essential feature was aerodynamics. This, in fact, was a good example of the form-follows-function principle — aerodynamic requirements set the parameters for the basic shape of the cars. Even though there was uneasiness about how America's mid-market car buyers would accept the radical new styling, there were simply too many practical benefits to the aeroshape. The more aerodynamic the style, the less wind resistance — or "drag" — the car encounters while in motion. The principle is known as "coefficient-of-drag" — "Cd" for short — and the lower the Cd number, the better. A compact car with a Cd of .36, for example, gets about two miles per gallon better highway mileage than a car of similar size with a .40 Cd. Most American cars in the early 1980s, with the exception of Ford's Thunderbird and LTD, had .48 Cds. The best standards up to that time had been developed in Europe, especially with the Mercedes-Benz and Audi 5000, which had .33 and .32 Cd ratings, respectively.

Ford's goal with the Taurus and Sable was to come as close to these pacesetting drag coefficients as possible. When the first models came out in December 1985, the ratings were .32 for the Sable sedan, .33 for the Tarus sedan, and .34 for both station wagons — all of which beat Ford's own best standard up to that time of .35 for the 1983 Thunderbird. The Cd ratings for the 1988 Taurus and Sable remain the same, but meanwhile Ford has brought the aerodynamics of several other product lines up to similar efficiency levels. The 1988 Lincoln Continental, for example, has a .36 rating; while the Thunderbird base model and the Scorpio have .34 coefficients; and the 1989 Probe boasts an outstanding .30 Cd.

Ford had also decided early in the program that the Taurus would be designed "from the inside out." A company press release proclaimed: "The driver is the focus for all engineering, design, performance, dynamics, and functions. The Taurus (and Sable) will be designed from the driver outward."

It might appear that the company was violating its own premise by predetermining the outer shape of the car and then designing it from the inside out. But that wasn't really the case; aerodynamic design had already been justified for both its functionalism and its driver-friendliness. The aeroshape not only delivered better gas mileage but also enhanced the handling and roadability of the car. Furthermore, it cut down on wind noise, thus giving the driver and passengers a quieter ride. In effect, the aeroshape already reflected a driver-focused design.

Ford, in any event, took the "driver-outward" design concept very seriously. Using ergonomics — the science of relationships between humans and machines — Team Taurus studied every facet of the driver's interaction with the car. The purpose was to give the driver complete control over the car — or, in other words, to "put the driver in the driver's seat." This meant designing a cockpit that brought all the instruments and control systems within quick and easy reach of the driver, making the job of driving as manageable as possible. Inherent in such a design is not only driver comfort but also *safety*. If all the fussy details that a driver has to attend to can be simplified, then the driver can pay more attention to watching the road, traffic signals, and other cars.

After considerable study, Team Taurus designed a cockpit with a slightly concave, or "swept-away," dashboard and instrument panel. This shape brought all the driver-related controls and instruments into clearer view and easier reach of the driver. Knobs, buttons, switches, and levers could all be seen at a glance and operated with a minimum of effort. In fact, the cockpit was designed so that once a new Taurus owner had driven the car just a few times, he or she could operate virtually every control merely by touch — without having to look away from the road and search for the right instrument.

Since drivers and passengers come in as many sizes and shapes as the human race affords, it is next to impossible to build a "universal" car seat that will comfortably fit everyone. But Team Taurus, aided by an unprecedented research investment in seat design, did about as good a job as could be expected in creating seats, both front and rear, that would conveniently accommodate a wide range of physical types. For one thing, front seats are offered in three configurations: (1) a full-length bench seat with a fold-down center armrest and a driver's seatback recliner that allows half-degree incremental adjustments; (2) a split-bench seat, with individual center fold-down armrests and dual seatback recliners; and (3) individual "bucket" recliner seats. All seats have lower-back supports and are made of heavy-density foam to help alleviate fatigue on long trips. And all front seats have headrests that adjust both horizontally and vertically. (The Sable also offers adjustable headrests for the rear seats — a first for an American car.)

At one point during its research, Ford learned of a common customer complaint involving the forward and backward floor-level adjustment of front seats. People said it was irritating to have to grope under the edge of the seat for a small release lever, which was located in different spots on different models of cars. It was especially inconvenient to people in two-car families, or people who frequently drove cars that didn't belong to them, such as rentals. Ford's ergonomical solution was to equip the Taurus with a horizontal release bar running almost the entire width of the seat beneath its front edge. The driver only needed to reach down, at any point, and the release bar would be there. Under the old Detroit philosophy there was a good chance that this improvement would *not* have been made. It would have been considered an insignificant detail affecting only a small number of drivers. And if it cost, say, an incremental $1.00 per car for a car that was expected to sell 500,000 units a year, then it would have been viewed as $500,000 in "lost" profit — maybe $2-3 million over the life span of the model.

But Ford was no longer thinking in such terms. Attention to detail was a cornerstone of the Team Taurus philosophy. As Lewis Veraldi put it, "We made sure that even the *common* things were done *uncommonly* well." What Team Taurus had discovered was that incorporating individual customer ideas about one part of the car or another — taking care of what Veraldi calls the "tremendous trifles" — enhanced customers' perceptions of the overall quality and comfort of the car.

The dual sun-visors offer a good example of a "common" feature that was treated in an "uncommon" way — although, really, the idea is very simple. Most late-model cars have adjustable sun-visors that can be swung to the front or to the side, depending on whether you're driving toward or parallel to the sun's glare. But in real life, streets and roads don't always run in straight lines for long distances. One moment, the sun is directly in front of you; the next, it may be directly to the side of you.

It is not only an inconvenience but also a compromise of driving safety to be constantly switching the visor as you follow the bends in the road. In the Taurus, however, dual visors block the sun's rays from both the front and side simultaneously, and built-in visor extensions offer further protection when the sun is low on the horizon.

Another detail that received uncommon attention was the coverage area of windshield wipers. Almost every car has blind spots on the windshield when it rains, simply because the wiper blades aren't long enough or positioned properly to give full coverage. The Taurus, however, was equipped with recessed 20-inch wiper blades that clear the water almost all the way to the driver's-side roof pillar, thus affording greater visibility than usual in rainy conditions. The windshield was also the focal point of an optional feature that can mean a great deal to drivers in northern climates. A patented electrical de-icer system manufactured by Ford's own glass operations and called Insta-Clear™ is capable of ridding the windshield of thick ice coatings in just three minutes in sub-zero weather.

Still another customer-friendly "trifle" is the use of a gas-operated hood-lifting mechanism that makes it easy to open the hood and leave it open without the aid of a prop rod.

In case after case, Team Taurus pursued similar customer-oriented ideas and opportunities — any one of which might have been viewed as relatively unimportant but which, taken together, added up to the most user-friendly car that Detroit had ever produced. The driver, for example, was given a left footrest and an oversized accelerator pedal for more comfort on long road trips. Cockpit controls were backlighted for easy visibility at night, and the map light was designed to give clear view to the front-seat passenger while remaining almost invisible to the driver. Rope netting was even installed in the trunk of the sedan, so that grocery bags could get from the supermarket to the driveway without falling over.

Aerodynamics, ergonomics, and driver/passenger "friendliness" — these were some of the vital, and un-Detroit-like, ingredients of the new cars Ford was betting its future on.

So, too, was the company's new and unrelenting commitment to quality. GM, or anybody else in the auto business, could design and build a car with an aerodynamic shape, or with ergonomically planned dashboards, seats, and brake pedals. But what would ultimately and definitively set the Taurus apart from its competition would be its overall quality in components, construction, and performance.

Quality can be a nebulous concept. If Ford was to build, not a "good" car, not a "better" car, but the "best"-quality car of its kind in the world, some objective standard of measurement was needed to help keep score. As with virtually everything else connected with the Taurus-Sable program, Ford had to invent its own standard. The result was the "Best-in-Class" program, or "BIC" for short.

The idea for BIC was not attributable to any one person, but arose from early brainstorming sessions among designers, engineers, and product specialists. Under the BIC program, the development team identified every major car in the world and then evaluated those cars in terms of 400 separate components, features, and functions. The key idea was not to rate every competitive car as a whole, but to evaluate each of the designated components or features on a car-by-car basis and to single out the best among them. The "best" then became Ford's target for the Taurus. The company would try to match or exceed the competition in as many of the 400 categories as possible.

BIC standards went beyond the usual issues of a car's performance, reliability, durability, and fit-and-finish. They also encompassed what Ford called "convenience and functional plusses to maximize customer value." The intent, said the company, was "to make the Taurus and Sable demonstrably better than competitive vehicles."

The 400 BIC items were grouped into twelve major categories and forty-nine sub-categories. The major areas covered were: ride, steering, handling, powertrain performance, powertrain smoothness, body chassis, performance feel, driveability, brakes, climate control, seat performance, and operational comfort.

Sub-categories covered an exhaustive list of functional as well as image-oriented features. Here are just a few of the specific items that the team studied:

- Turning diameter
- Driver's rearward visibility
- Gear noise
- Brake-lining life
- Brake-pedal height
- Steering-wheel feel
- Foot-control ergonomics
- Squeaks and rattles
- Speedometer accuracy
- Ease of checking brake fluid
- Side-door closing sound
- Glove compartment size and accessibility
- Size and shape of the headlight switch
- Size of the outside rear-view mirror
- Ignition key size and weight
- Driver's left foot comfort
- Driver's right foot comfort

The team even measured the number of times you had to turn the handle to roll a manually operated window up and down. The Mazda 626 won best-in-class for this particular function. It took four turns to crank down the Mazda's front windows, and three and three-quarters turns to handle the rear windows. This sterling performance, however, was beyond the reach of the Taurus. BIC couldn't be achieved in the manual window-cranking competition with Mazda. But the reason for this "failure" illustrates a quite serious issue in car design. Ford's BIC evaluators explained that the "more severe curvature of [Taurus's] flush glass does not allow BIC to be achieved for number of turns." In other words, there was a trade-off. The aerodynamic styling of the Taurus required that the windows be flush with the car's rounded body, and this obviously meant that the window glass had to be curved to an unusual degree. The result was a somewhat less efficient window-cranking system — a problem that most people might consider minor, but that Ford would make an effort to modify in later models of the Taurus.

In any case, this particular BIC conflict reflects the complexity of designing a car as an integrated totality. Change one thing, and you'll most likely have to change a number of others. And if you don't follow up with those changes, you'll end up with a hodge-podge — a jerry-built piece of machinery in which many of the components work at cross purposes. Unfortunately, this had been the case with too many Detroit products for many years.

The first Taurus released in December 1985 met the target on 320 of the 400 selected BIC features — in other words, it matched or bettered a full *80 percent* of the best features found on the best cars of its class in the world. By combining the BIC concept with other research, ergonomics, and true teamwork, Ford brought a "whole" product to market — whole in the sense of synergistically uniting in one car many of the best possible automotive features without having them cancel one another out.

It was all well and good that Ford was on track in developing its new world-class cars and in evolving a new corporate culture. But at the start of the 1980s the company's production facilities were also in serious need of attention. In fact, the Taurus couldn't be built — certainly not at the intended quality level or with the necessary cost-effectiveness — unless plants were overhauled and new technology was installed.

A certain amount of retooling and revision of assembly-line procedures was always necessary to bring out a new car. But the Taurus was so drastically different from other Ford products that more than the usual changes were in order. It wasn't so much a matter of the new aerodynamic body style; Ford was already retooling for that. Long before the Taurus and Sable were to go into production, the company would bring out the aerostyled 1983 Thunderbird, Cougar, Tempo, Topaz, and the Lincoln Mark VII. What made the Taurus so much more demanding was that beneath its aerostyled exterior it was a totally new car that required new techniques and standards in assembly. It not only contained over 4,000 newly designed components, but its targeted quality level demanded greater manufacturing precision, tighter process controls, and finer attention to detail. Before the Taurus program, Ford typically did only a single "audit" of a new car prior to job one. That's when the engineers, product specialists, and manufacturing experts made one final detailed inspection of the car and the assembly lines. With the Taurus and Sable, however, Ford did *six* pre-production audits to try to ensure that every hitch and glitch had been eliminated. Management wanted to be sure not only that the cars' form and function were right but also that their fit and finish measured up to the world-class standards Ford had set.

General Motors' heavy investment in new technology and manufacturing facilities rather than in new cars may not have been as strategically astute as Ford's concentration on developing its new products. Nevertheless, Ford simply *had* to "fix up the farm," so to speak, or those new products could never become a reality. Interestingly, in Ford's 1981 annual report, only one 19-line paragraph was devoted to the subject of "Manufacturing Advances," and not a single photograph was shown featuring plant facilities or manufacturing technology. Three years later, however, the 1984 annual report waxed enthusiastic on the subject of "Manufacturing Technology," devoting to it 175 lines of copy accompanied by six vivid color photographs of high-tech production equipment and processes.

In 1984 — and even in early 1988, when the Taurus was well into its third model year — Ford still had a long way to go in renovating its plants and introducing new technology. But the company had nonetheless made big strides in the meantime.

The Atlanta and Chicago plants, where the Taurus and Sable were being assembled, showed major improvements, especially in the areas of automated systems and robotics. Even in the early design and engineering stages, computers had been used more extensively on the Taurus than on any previous Ford product, and by 1987, computer-assisted design and computer-aided manufacturing (CAD-CAM) had become the norm at Ford. The metal-stamping process for the Taurus was controlled by the most advanced CAD-CAM system in the world, and robots performed 94 percent of the spot welds on the car. Electronic test probes were also used to monitor the integrity of body construction, and automated trolleys contributed greatly to efficiency all along the assembly line. Electronic probes, in fact, were used throughout the manufacturing process to ensure that design and engineering specifications were being met and to verify the quality, fit, and dimensional stability of every component and subsystem on the car.

In addition to computers, robots, and automated trolleys, the Taurus assembly lines showed another distinctly new look. Individual workers were no longer strung out in a straight line, each performing a single rote (and boring) function. Instead, production *teams* worked on whole modules or sub-assemblies of the cars. This, of course, was an extension of the team philosophy adopted overall by Ford in 1979. One benefit was to bring workers together in groups where they shared a common team objective. With a few necessary exceptions involving highly individual and specialized functions, production employees no longer stood isolated, performing an endlessly repetitive task.

Another benefit recalls the time-worn adage, "two heads are better than one." With several workers collaborating on a whole sub-system, there was a greater likelihood that someone in the group would detect any potential problem while it was still feasible to take corrective action. In other words, it was less likely that a defect in a component or module would proceed on down the line to be compounded or covered up at later stages in the car's assembly.

This arrangement also worked well with an assembly-line innovation that Ford was the first to introduce in American carmaking. Called the "stop-line" system, it was a technique pioneered by the Japanese that would have been unthinkable in Detroit in the pre-Taurus era. It was simply a matter of allowing any worker who detected a problem along the assembly line to stop the entire line. Naturally, there would be a concern that some workers might abuse this prerogative, either intentionally or simply by mistake. But the watchword at Ford now was *teamwork* — and this, along with other new policies and programs, called for a new level of trust and mutual respect among management, technicians, supervisors, and line workers. Ford had to trust its people; and by offering that trust, the company was inviting workers to take — and enjoy — a higher level of pride and satisfaction in their work.

Still another very important assembly-line innovation introduced with the Taurus was called the "doors-off" procedure. In the past, the fully assembled and painted shell of a vehicle moved down the line with its doors open to permit the installation of dashboards, seats, and other interior components and trim. This was an unwieldy process because the open doors got in the way of workers. Furthermore, it exposed the doors to possible dents and scratches, and sometimes the doors could even become sprung or misaligned. In tooling up for the Taurus, Ford developed a system by which the doors are removed from the vehicle before it starts down the trim line, leaving easy access for trim workers and protecting the doors from possible damage. The complete set of doors for each vehicle is picked up and attached to an overhead conveyor, which moves along at the same pace as the rest of the line. When all the interior work is finished on the car, its own set of doors is waiting at the end of the trim line to be re-attached. The cost-effectiveness of the system is obvious. It not only reduces the number of defective doors but also makes the trim workers' jobs easier and faster. In fact, it made so much sense that General Motors announced it would begin using the doors-off method in its new Saturn assembly operations.

Other improvements that were needed before the Taurus could be produced included expansion and modernization of the Atlanta assembly plant. Ford built a new 144,000-square-foot body shop and a 207,000-square-foot paint facility. The paint shop was a free-standing building, set apart from other manufacturing facilities to minimize contamination from dirt, dust, and metal scrapings. It was also designed to be tight and as environmentally suitable as possible to the task, with built-in temperature, humidity, and anti-dust controls.

The most telling measures of productivity are the number of cars that come off the assembly line per hour and the number of workers it takes to make them. That's assuming, of course, that you're talking about *good* cars — cars that won't have to be diverted to repair stations to have defects corrected before they can leave the plant. Ford had dealt with the quality-control factor from just about every conceivable angle, after recognizing that productivity improvement and quality were not mutually exclusive aspirations. "In reality," Don Petersen said, "quality and productivity are two sides of the same coin." But the question remained: could the new cars be produced at a reasonably fast pace without adding to payroll costs? Before the Taurus came along, the Atlanta plant was producing fifty cars per hour with approximately 2,600 employees; but in the first year of Taurus and Sable production, Atlanta brought out sixty-three cars per hour with the same number of workers. In Chicago the story was virtually the same. The Windy City plant had been producing fifty-three cars per hour in pre-Taurus days, but in 1988 it turned out the same number as Atlanta — sixty-three — representing almost a 20 percent increase in productivity with no addition to the work force. Just as important, more of the cars coming off the lines were good cars. Before the Taurus program, as many as ten to fifteen of every hundred cars built in Ford plants had to be diverted for repairs after assembly. But from 1979 to 1988, the company steadily reduced this cripple rate — first to five cars per hundred, and eventually to just one or two.

Ford's "bet" was paying off. It is important to remember, however, that the company's commitment to quality was made long before such success could be assured. The "new" look of the Taurus had given Ford executives many anxious moments in the early 1980s. Knowing that the aeroshape was functionally right didn't negate the concern that America's mid-market drivers might turn their backs on it — with devastating consequences for the company. Even some of the respected writers and editors for automotive magazines — people who are usually receptive to new and innovative ideas — were skeptical. They could easily understand the functional benefits of aerostyling, but some of them felt that it was more appropriate for futuristic "concept" cars than for family sedans and station wagons. Furthermore, even if the style caught on, what would happen when Ford's competitors started copying it?

When Jack Telnack was showing early design sketches to magazine representatives, one editor quipped that if aerodynamic design was so efficient, then everybody would start using it and all cars would look alike. Telnack's reply was, "All birds are aerodynamically shaped, but you can still tell a canary from an eagle."

5

Better Ideas
from Within

The road from the styling studio to the dealer's showroom floor is always a long road for any new car to travel. For the Taurus it was all the longer because nobody in the United States had ever traveled this particular road before. It wasn't even on the maps.

Long before the drawings of the Taurus had emerged from Ford's design studios, many separate activities had been set in motion to pave the way for the new cars. In the process, the Ford Motor Company was to undergo radical changes that would have implications far beyond the fate of the Taurus-Sable program and would help forge new relationships both inside and outside the company. The corporate culture of the company would be fundamentally altered, and new ways of thinking about old problems and old relationships would be adopted.

From the very start of the Taurus-Sable program, every policy, method, process, and activity normally involved in the creation of a new car was called into question. Nothing was taken for granted and nothing was held sacred, including the traditional authoritarian role of management. The team concept — itself a drastic break from tradition — required that people communicate and collaborate in a manner that was totally foreign to the American car industry. Barriers of rank and job classification had to be breached, and people had to be persuaded to speak out and to listen. At the heart of the new strategy was *attitude change*, and Philip Caldwell meant for the new attitudes to be infused throughout the company — from World Headquarters to the assembly lines.

American manufacturers had been grumbling for years about how uncooperative and counterproductive their unionized work forces had become. It was assumed, for example, that the superior quality of Japanese cars and the greater productivity of Japanese factories were largely due to a more efficient and dedicated work force. Japanese workers, it was said, took greater pride in their work, while too many Americans showed up at the plant merely to punch the time clock and go through minimal motions until the end of their shift.

Unfortunately, there was a degree of truth in this. But as the Taurus-Sable program moved ahead, Ford was to find that its workers weren't nearly as jaded or recalcitrant as they'd been made out to be. American autoworkers could be as productive as any in the world, but they had to be recognized as *allies* and had to be given a chance to participate fully in the job at hand. Obviously, this required attitude changes on all sides — something that was far easier to talk about than to bring about. After all, U.S. industry had traditionally viewed its line workers as quantitative *costs*, not as qualitative *assets*. As Philip Caldwell was to admit in retrospect, the American industrial worker was most often regarded by management as "a single-purpose machine tool." This view of labor, however, was on its way out at Ford in the late seventies. "We had realized by then," said Caldwell, "that if you have 300,000 or so people in the company, it only makes good sense to have *all* of their brains working for you."

In Detroit, as in other American industrial sectors, management and organized labor had been confirmed antagonists for years. This was somewhat less the case with Ford than with the other U.S. automakers, especially in the upper echelons of company and union leadership, but there was still a gulf between the two sides. Throughout the industry, mutual trust and respect were exceptions to the rule. Corporate executives and union leaders barely spoke the same language, and the resulting communication gap became even wider inside the factories, where line workers didn't speak management's language either. The inevitable result was that workers paid greater allegiance to their union than they did to their company. This was certainly nothing new or startling. It simply reflected the way in which industrial relations had evolved in the United States.

What was new at the start of the 1980s, however, was a fresh determination by Ford to bring the United Auto Workers (UAW) into a closer partnership with management for the sake of a *common* cause: saving the company. The best car design, the best engineering, and all the advanced manufacturing technology available wouldn't produce a world-class car without the cooperation of the line worker. This meant that the traditional adversarial relationship between union and management had to be softened, and the company had to find ways to communicate more directly and more effectively with the people who worked its assembly lines.

After he became president at Ford, Donald Petersen called in a consultant who was legendary in Japan for the contributions he had made to the Japanese auto industry. Ironically, this man — W. Edwards Deming — was an American, and he had gone to the aid of the Japanese more than twenty years earlier, after the U.S. auto industry had snubbed his carmaking ideas. Petersen and other Ford executives wanted Deming to reveal the "secrets" of how the Japanese built such high-quality cars. They were surprised, however, when Deming refused to deal directly with automotive quality and insisted on talking instead about Ford's management philosophy and corporate culture. Deming told the Ford executives flatly that only about 20 percent of the company's quality problem could be laid to the workers, while 80 percent had to do with management's attitudes and values, as well as its methods, procedures, and systems. It was management, after all, that determined the manufacturing processes, set the production schedules, and decided when and where money would be spent on the physical plant. In other words, management itself was responsible for the bulk of the problem.

While Deming's candid, face-to-face indictment of management on the issue of quality might have been both surprising and embarrassing to the Ford executives, they nonetheless took him seriously. It was still quite early in the company's turnaround program, but the new mood among key executives was to listen and to be critically objective — even if it sometimes hurt. As Ford executive Peter Pestillo would say in 1983, when he was vice president for labor relations, the company had to begin its turnaround by "recognizing and accepting the fact that our traditional management system had grown stale; the hierarchical-dictating approach had lost its effectiveness. It didn't require an obituary to convince us it was in need of fixing."

The workers and their union, however, couldn't be let off the hook entirely. By continuously driving up wages and benefits, the UAW had forced management to look for ways to cut other costs and to boost production. Cost-cutting was often achieved at the sacrifice of equipment maintenance and with the postponement of badly needed capital improvements in the plants. To increase output, management set higher quotas, pushing the workers to produce at a faster pace. The objective was to run the lines as fast as possible; the results were disgruntled workers and a high rate of defective products.

At one Ford engine plant during the late seventies, for example, the quota was 300 engines per hour. But as many as 40 to 50 percent of those engines were defective and had to be either scrapped or shunted off to repair stations. By 1987, as a result of the many new policies instituted during the Taurus-Sable program, that same plant produced "only" 175-200 engines per hour. But there were far fewer defects, and the company actually got more usable engines at the lower hourly quota.

In the meantime, complicated union work rules that had been accumulating over the years had led to excessive job specialization. By the late seventies, this meant that some workers labored at a breakneck pace while others read magazines and newspapers, caught a nap, or stood around telling jokes — all on company time. Under the circumstances, morale and productivity had to be joking matters as well, and it was difficult to see how workers could have any pride in their jobs or respect for their company.

Such deep-seated problems wouldn't yield to simplistic measures. A handful of workers might momentarily respond to a catchy, rah-rah slogan or an impassioned plea to their conscience. A few more might be honestly intrigued by the idea of building a truly good car for a change. But most would still think first about their paychecks and job security. Everybody knew that jobs were disappearing in the domestic car industry, but many people who still held their jobs were caught up in a sort of group lassitude. It was as though nothing could be done to *really* improve matters, so you simply held onto your job for as long as it was there. And if anything could indeed be done, it would probably be done by the government — either with more Chrysler-style bailouts or with import-bashing trade restrictions. Meanwhile, management always seemed to be sounding alarms, demanding wage cuts or freezes, or making grandiose vows about improving quality and becoming more competitive. When Ford first told its workers about the company's new no-nonsense plan to upgrade quality and build a world-class car, the reactions ranged from bored skepticism to scornful disbelief. "We've heard that sort of talk before" was the standard *polite* reply.

Ford management, however, did more than just talk. In 1979, the company instituted a program called Employee Involvement (EI). The program was based on the idea that — in the words of Peter Pestillo — "those closest to the problem may also be closest to the solution." Union or nonunion, hourly or salaried, supervisor or line worker — all Ford employees were invited to participate in the EI program on a voluntary basis. Employees met on company time in groups of ten to twelve people from the same job unit — interior trim, seat installation, painting, and so on — to air complaints and offer problem-solving ideas.

Of course, such "involvement" groups often amount to little more than game-playing if management doesn't take them seriously or if the union doesn't back them. In Ford's case, not only did management take EI seriously, but the UAW endorsed it from the beginning. The union's quick acceptance of EI came partly because the idea was a familiar one. In 1972 GM had created an EI-like program called "quality of work life" (QWL). Over the years, GM has invested heavily in QWL, with reportedly good results. Another such effort, called "job enrichment," was launched at Chrysler in 1973, but with less success. Doug Fraser, then president of the UAW, notes that the Chrysler program never went far because the company had so many other problems at the time. "What Ford has done," says Fraser, "is to actually make employee involvement *work.*" "The Ford program took off on a more uniform basis, and the company has proliferated the idea and given it better form and direction."

In a surprisingly short time after EI was introduced, Ford was reaping not only better employee morale but also concrete results through cost-saving suggestions, improved production methods, and higher product quality.

EI groups at the Louisville, Kentucky truck assembly plant in 1981 assisted in design reviews for the 1983 Ranger pickup truck, and hundreds of their suggestions were adopted. In 1982 employees at Oakville, Ontario and Kansas City, Missouri submitted 666 ideas for improving manufacturing methods or upgrading quality on the 1984 Tempo and Topaz. The company adopted more than three-fourths of these suggestions. As the Taurus program moved forward, Ford came to rely more and more heavily on such direct, factory-level input from its employees.

Perhaps not surprisingly, Ford's adoption of so many of the suggestions was itself to become the basic "incentive" to keep employees interested in the EI program. There were no cash bonuses or other financial incentives to participate, but the psychic satisfaction — pride, status, involvement in a common effort — proved to be incentive enough. Initially, Ford seems to have promoted the program by convincing many employees that the company's very survival — and the survival of their jobs — depended on their involvement. But once their efforts were taken seriously, most people, as Philip Caldwell has said, simply *wanted* to do the right thing — and wanted to do good work, given half a chance.

More than four years before the scheduled start of Taurus production, the company began sending teams of executives, designers, and engineers to its Atlanta, Georgia, assembly plant, the first of the two plants where the new cars would be built. The purpose of these trips — which would total fourteen by the time the first Taurus came off the line — was to solicit ideas from the Atlanta employees. In effect, management was going to the factory floor and asking supervisors and line workers how to build a better car and how to build it more efficiently. This was an unheard-of practice in the American auto industry. Detroit management, Ford's included, had always ruled by decree from the top down, and ideas that originated in the lower reaches of a company had typically been ignored or suppressed.

With that kind of history, it was to be expected that not every production employee in Atlanta would be duly impressed with the seriousness of the visits. But the payoff was not long in coming. Ford soon discovered that its Atlanta factory employees were a rich source of innovative and practical ideas. The workers contributed more than 1,400 recommendations, and over 700 of them were actually adopted. Proof was emerging that the American autoworker was not, after all, permanently out to lunch.

Some of the recommendations by plant employees were so simple that it's hard to understand why nobody in Detroit had thought of them before. For example, a body-shop supervisor — a twenty-five-year veteran of Ford — questioned why three different welding guns were needed to attach the firewall to the body of the Taurus. The three separate guns, suspended by cable from overhead, got in the workers' way and slowed down the operation. Taking the supervisor's suggestion to heart, engineers designed a single gun to weld all the way across the cowling-firewall assembly, thus saving production time and lessening the potential for errors and accidents.

Another employee suggestion that paid off handsomely involved the assembly of the body side and door-opening panels. The Ford LTD and Mercury Marquis — which were to be replaced by the Taurus and Sable — had nine separate panels that had to be fitted together on the factory floor to complete the body side and doors. Original plans for the Taurus and Sable called for a reduction to six panels. An Atlanta employee noted, however, that if the number of panels could be reduced even further, it would not only save assembly time but also allow for a better fit and finish. With fewer separate parts to be joined on the assembly line, there would be fewer chances for poor alignment, and the side of the car would be smoother and tighter. Again, the engineers went back to the drawing board, and this time they designed a side-assembly consisting of just *two* panels.

There were many more cost-saving, quality-enhancing suggestions that originated with shop employees and line supervisors. The majority of them were small, relatively undramatic improvements involving perhaps the elimination of a bolt here and there, or a slight change in procedure on the line. Taken cumulatively, however, employee recommendations had an immeasurable effect on the eventual success of the Taurus. And throughout the company, the EI program had a profound impact on cost savings, better product quality, improved communications, and higher morale.

It isn't feasible to provide an exhaustive list of EI success stories, but here are just a few additional examples:

- At the Louisville plant, chrome trim from an outside supplier often came wrinkled because of poor packing for shipment. Louisville employees visited the supplier and suggested better packaging methods. The results were cost savings and better assurance of uniform quality in the chrome trim.
- When Ford's Aerostar minivan was in design, a plant worker told an engineer that an access hole in a door was too small. The worker would have to reach through the hole to screw in a bolt, and the tight squeeze would cause some bolts to be dropped inside the door, where they couldn't be retrieved. The amazingly simple solution was

to make the hole a little larger, and the result was that far fewer Aerostars went to market with loose bolts rattling around inside the doors.

- Viewing a prototype of the Taurus, a worker noted that a certain bolt on the hood assembly seemed superfluous. Indeed, it was — and so it was designed out of the car, saving a little money on bolts, cutting a few seconds of production time per car, and leaving one less component that might malfunction.

- In Atlanta, workers asked why it was necessary to use several different sizes of screws to fasten interior plastic moldings on the Taurus. The diversity of screws meant frequent changing of the heads on torquing power tools. Engineers agreed that a single size of screw would do just as well. The result: minutes saved in production time per car and a simpler inventory of screws.

In 1986, Peter Pestillo estimated that a typical employee recommendation adopted under the EI program saved the company anywhere from $300,000 to $700,000. But that is only part of the story. The company adopted a few recommendations that actually cost money but contributed to better product quality. And in any case, the success of a program like EI is hard to measure strictly in dollar terms. How, for example, do you place a dollar value on a gradual and cumulative improvement in employee morale? The elements of a corporate culture are ideas and feelings — *qualities*, not quantities. This was the Ford Motor Company's important discovery, a fact that had long been overlooked in Detroit and elsewhere in American industry. Ford's focus now was on the *value* of its products, and on the value and *values* of its people.

The ways in which the company measured value were also different. The value of a car did not lie in its sticker price, or in the money invested to build it. Value had to do, instead, with the car's styling, engineering, quality of construction, faithfulness to purpose, and satisfaction to its owner. Likewise, the values of Ford's people were seen in a different light. Certainly, pay scales and benefits represented concrete, quantitative matters that had to be dealt with; but that's not all there was to having a qualified and dependable work force. The employees' satisfaction with their workplace, pride of workmanship, respect for coworkers and management, and sense of belonging to a team and having their ideas count for something — these qualitative determinants of the company's productivity, competitiveness, and profitability were all equally important.

In 1983 Ford did try to "quantify" its progress on this front by conducting a survey of EI participants, and the numbers are impressive. Of the 750 employees polled, 82 percent reported satisfaction with their jobs — compared with 58 percent of Ford employees reporting job satisfaction before EI was instituted. Perhaps more significant was the 82 percent who indicated they had a chance to accomplish something worthwhile, in contrast to the 27 percent who felt that way in the pre-EI days. It's natural to assume that these figures reflect the enthusiasm of participants over nonparticipants. But that enthusiasm was clearly infectious, as reflected by a reduction in the number of job grievances filed. By 1983, the grievance rate had gone down by as much as 75 percent at some Ford plants.

The Employee Involvement program at Ford thus was not some Mickey Mouse industrial-relations gimmick dreamed up to fill bulletin-board posters or to generate trade press publicity. It was a *real* effort to tap resources that had long been underutilized, if not totally ignored: the ideas, experience, and brass-tacks knowledge of the people who worked in the shops. A familiar Ford advertising slogan had proclaimed for several years that "Ford has a better idea!" Although that slogan was coined before the EI program was created, the "better ideas" were indeed there all along, and they weren't confined to the Glass House or the design and engineering studios. They also flourished at supervisors' stations and along the assembly lines in Ford's factories.

Gaining the trust, enlisting the cooperation, and tapping the knowledge of plant workers could be only partly accomplished through a formal company-sponsored program such as EI. There were still those cynical or indifferent employees who wouldn't respond to such efforts. As Philip Caldwell put it, "There are always a few bad apples, but you don't want to organize your whole company to accommodate those exceptions." There were also those who would listen to nobody but the union. The UAW, then, held an important high card in Ford's bet-the-ranch showdown.

Ford's relations with the UAW had been fairly peaceful since the post-World War II era. There had been disputes and even a few strikes, including a damaging strike in 1967, but Henry Ford II — in contrast to his fiercely antiunion grandfather — was known for his social conscience and enlightened attitude toward workers. While he was running the company from 1945 to 1979, UAW officials typically looked first to Ford when they wanted to focus on nonmonetary issues. If a big wage hike was on the union's agenda, they would target GM or Chrysler for a possible strike, in order to set an industrywide wage pattern. But when it came to what they considered the "human" issues, such as working conditions or job security, they felt they could negotiate more successfully with Ford. Thus, while UAW officials and Ford executives obviously did not share the same mind-set, there was nonetheless a better basis for union-management communication and cooperation at Ford than there was at the other auto companies. Both sides still had their hard-liners, but both sides also had people who were willing to listen to new ideas.

In 1981 UAW and Ford negotiators traveled together to Japan to see first-hand how the Japanese automakers operated. Even making such a joint trip was, in itself, an example of how labor and management at Ford were trying to be more cooperative than adversarial. The assault by Japanese imports threatened the interests of management and workers alike, and in both a symbolic and a realistic sense, the trip signaled a united front by one of America's oldest and biggest industrial firms and one of its most powerful labor unions. On this occasion, at least, labor and management were marching shoulder to shoulder. They had a common enemy, and they needed to learn something about that enemy's tactics. What were the secrets of Japanese labor-management peace? Was it simply a matter of cultural differences, or were the Japanese doing things that could be adopted in the United States?

Leading Ford's management contingent for this trip was Peter Pestillo. His union counterpart on the visit was Donald Ephlin, a top official and negotiator in the Ford department of the UAW. In a short time, these two men would again face each other across the bargaining table. As it turned out, their ideas would be instrumental in crafting new labor contracts in 1982 and 1984 that would ease the financial pressures on Ford and contribute vitally to the turnaround in the company's corporate culture. Ephlin, in fact, would incur the ire of UAW hard-liners by recommending concessions on wages and cost-of-living increases in exchange for better job security and a greater union role in plant-closing decisions. Doug Fraser points out that, except for the Chrysler rescue effort, the UAW in its entire history had never granted such major concessions as it did with Ford in 1982. "We made wage and benefit concessions worth some $1.2 billion over the life of the contract," he notes. "But Ford workers, more so than GM's, recognized the real competitive problems the industry was facing. Most of them understood that Ford had to have some cost relief, and when we took the issues to them and convinced them of what the company was trying to do, over 70 percent of them voted to accept the contract." Neither did it hurt, according to Fraser, that Ford for some years had earned a reputation for playing straight with the union and taking an honest interest in its workers.

The contracts negotiated in 1982 and 1984 represented milestones in Ford's recovery effort, and they reflected a growing spirit of conciliation and accommodation between union and management. The 1982 contract was not only negotiated in a record-setting thirteen days, but it was concluded six months before the old contract expired. Ephlin may have risked his stature as a union pro, but Ford negotiators also gave up some treasured company prerogatives by allowing the union a greater voice in the size and makeup of the work force and in the shaping of the company's physical plant.

The joint trip to Japan should not be overestimated in its importance, but it nonetheless yielded some useful ideas and insights that could influence the thinking back in Detroit. Pestillo, for example, reported one episode that led him to rethink his own role and that of the office he held. He asked a Japanese plant manager how he divided his time between "labor relations" and "general personnel activities" — and the Japanese manager couldn't answer! To him, there was no difference; labor relations and personnel administration were one and the same thing.

From this response, Pestillo said he learned that negotiating labor contracts and settling union grievances were not the be-all and end-all of dealing with the work force. Ford, he said, needed to pay even more attention to its workers' interests outside of the formally structured union-company relationship. Sticking to the letter of the labor contract was not enough anymore. Doing only what the company *had* to do told employees, in effect, that they were entitled only to what the union had been able to squeeze out of the company. That sort of thinking served to reinforce the "us-versus-them" attitudes that blocked effective communication between managers and hourly workers. The company, said Pestillo, should concentrate on doing what was *right* instead of doing merely what was contractually required. The importance of the EI program in accomplishing these goals cannot be overemphasized, in Pestillo's view, because it "shifted the emphasis from labor relations to human relations."

It certainly didn't happen overnight, nor even after the negotiation of the landmark labor contracts in 1982 and 1984; but gradually, Ford management and the union grew more empathetic toward each other. Management recognized that hourly workers had more to contribute than just their time and sweat, or, as Don Petersen put it, Ford had to "involve their hearts and minds in their jobs, and not just their backs and muscles." Ford's success in doing this was borne out by the response from workers in Atlanta, Louisville, Kansas City, and elsewhere when they were asked to offer advice and suggestions. And when management actually adopted many of those suggestions, it was proof to employees that they could be appreciated for more than their muscle alone. Slowly but steadily, the EI program attracted more and more employees as they became convinced that management was dead serious about turning the company around, and equally serious about listening to their ideas.

There did happen to be a few union officials who resisted the EI program because they felt that it came between them and their members. If union solidarity was to be preserved, it was dangerous to let management and the workers get *too* close, or to let management enlist workers in joint activities that were not strictly controlled by the union. Furthermore, since EI groups brought people together outside the routine pattern of work assignments, it threatened to disassemble the elaborate system of job classifications and work rules that the UAW had painfully constructed over the years.

Despite such objections, there were enough persuasive voices, both in the union and in management, to convince an ever-growing number of employees that there was no alternative but to begin cooperating. The company was on the line — and with it, the jobs of everybody concerned, whether they carried a union card or not.

In 1981 the principle of worker-management cooperation was put to a hard test at a Ford stamping plant in Walton Hills, Ohio, just outside Cleveland. Ford management had decided in 1980 that the company had one too many stamping plants, and since the Walton Hills operation had a very bad record for quality and productivity, it was the one ticketed for closing. The Cleveland area has long been a stronghold of militant unionism, and labor relations at the Walton Hills plant in 1980-81 were about as bad as they could get. Both sides had to share the blame, however. Plant management at Walton Hills often tended to be arrogant, stubborn, and heavy-handed; and many of the unionized workers responded with resentment and open hostility. This union-management antagonism had fed upon itself until it became what one Ford executive described as "guerrilla warfare."

In the circumstances, it was understandable that Ford wanted to get out of Walton Hills. Poor quality and low productivity seemed to offer justification enough, and for a company that was staking its survival in large part upon a new spirit of cooperation, the Walton Hills situation might have looked too far gone to be turned around. But when Ford said the plant was to be shut down, it was a union voice that pleaded for cooperation. Ken Bannon of the UAW's Ford department appealed to Philip Caldwell, Don Petersen, and Red Poling, and he successfully argued for one last chance to save the plant. Bannon and the head of the UAW local at Walton Hills — Joseph D'Amico — then worked out a survival plan. Their plan did not contain any "gifts" to the workers. The immediate incentive for employees would be simply the preservation of their jobs, and to accomplish this, they would have to give up some of the union's cushy work rules that had been undercutting quality and eating into productivity.

At the start, Bannon and D'Amico stood almost alone. The other officers of the union local opposed their plan, and many of the workers balked at the idea of ceding anything to the company. One Walton Hills hourly employee described the early stages of the plant rescue effort as "a war about to happen." There were those rank-and-file members, he said, who were honestly concerned that the proposed plan would erode legitimate union strength. But there were also the strident, combative voices of people who are seldom willing to listen but are almost always spoiling for a fight. When D'Amico started talking about work-rule concessions, this employee said, the mood of many workers turned ugly, and there were threats of a wildcat strike.

Nevertheless, once the message got across that Ford really intended to shut the plant down, more than 80 percent of the local members voted to accept the proposal. With the new work rules in place, Ford then launched an EI program at Walton Hills. There were no dramatic, overnight changes, but workers gradually took more interest in their jobs and began making useful suggestions. The company reciprocated by treating workers with more respect and by honestly listening to what they had to say. As employees saw their ideas and those of their coworkers being put into practice, many of them noticeably demonstrated more pride in their work. Quality and productivity inched upward, and top management acknowledged the improvements by restoring jobs that had been cut earlier. From a work force of about 1,600 in 1981, the plant's hourly payroll climbed back to more than 2,200 people in 1988.

While, admittedly, change was slow in coming at Walton Hills, it should be noted that the plant had a long way to come. For an operation that appeared doomed, and for a work force that had been virtually at war with the company, the very fact that the plant was still open in 1988 reflected a significant accomplishment. Furthermore, it was a tribute not only to the new worker-involvement philosophy at Ford but also to the imagination and courage of two union leaders and of those Walton Hills employees who decided early on to give Ford's idea a chance to work.

Attitudes did indeed change at Walton Hills. By 1987, EI groups at the plant were even designing new assembly lines — a project calling for a level of cooperation that nobody would have dreamed possible a few years earlier. Also in 1987, Ford gave the Walton Hills operation a new vote of confidence by investing $90 million in the plant to produce exterior body parts for the restyled Thunderbird and Cougar scheduled for introduction in 1989.

Nonetheless, in 1988 there remains a faction of recalcitrant workers at the plant. An estimated one or two of every ten workers cling to their old attitudes and refuse to accept what is going on around them. Described by one employee as "the type who're *never* satisfied," these people still hold the power to undermine the hard-won achievements of their coworkers. Unless productivity and product quality continue to improve at Walton Hills, Ford could decide once again to pull out.

Another key element in Ford's recovery strategy was the elimination of excess manufacturing capacity. Some of the plants were going to be closed — period. Ordinarily, one might have expected that only the older, physically deteriorating plants would be vulnerable. But not so under the new thinking at Ford. The plants with lingering problems of poor quality and uncooperative workers were the ones with uncertain futures. The company made this very clear early in the turnaround program when economics and production planning dictated that it choose one of two East Coast plants for shutdown. A relatively new plant in New Jersey was closed in 1980 because it had a bad quality record, while an aging plant in Virginia was kept open because its product quality rated much higher.

This decision was widely publicized throughout the company as evidence that Ford was totally committed to higher standards of quality. Overhauling physical facilities and introducing new technology would also be important, but when a newer plant was scrapped and an older one maintained, the overt message was: Performance is what counts. And implicitly, Ford was sending a signal that *people* made more of a difference than physical facilities.

The "people" theme recurs again and again throughout Ford's renaissance story. "Employee involvement is our way of life," states a Ford ad in a trade magazine. "We are a team. We must treat each other with trust and respect. What this means is that everyone at Ford is involved like never before in bringing a new car to market. Whether that person is an executive or assembly worker, his or her opinions and suggestions are actively sought. Nobody's input is ignored."

That's fine for an advertisement. It makes the company look good, and it's the kind of copy public relations people love to write. Ford's advertising rhetoric, however, does not seem to be mere puffery; the evidence indicates that Ford is indeed practicing what it preaches. A Walton Hills employee affirmed in late 1987 that the workers who *wanted* to go along with the company were being given every chance to do so. "This new approach is definitely for real," he said.

In 1986 Lewis Veraldi told a University of Michigan management seminar: "You have to decentralize authority and give people some control over their destiny. The philosophy behind employee involvement says that someone who is involved and who *cares* also needs the ability to *do* something about it."

Veraldi noted that the designs for Taurus headlight assemblies were modified through suggestions from plant-level employees to produce a cleaner, more symmetrical look regardless of how the lights are adjusted. "Designs like this don't happen by accident," he said. "Someone's idea triggered an action that improved a small design detail — and that's what employee involvement is all about."

The seriousness with which Ford is crediting plant employees' judgment and seeking their involvement is also borne out by at least two other departures from tradition. At Taurus and Sable plants, hourly workers have the authority to pick up the phone and consult directly with supplier executives if they discover problems or want to make suggestions. And throughout the Ford organization, as mentioned earlier, the "stop-line" procedure gives individual workers on the assembly line the power to stop the entire line on their own initiative if they detect a problem.

Giving hourly employees such latitude was unthinkable in the Ford of yesterday but is routine in the Ford of today. And while implementing new policies like these hasn't always meant a silky smooth ride for the organization, this aspect of Ford's new corporate culture appears to have paid off beyond the expectations of Philip Caldwell, Don Petersen, and Red Poling.

Not all of it has come about, however, from the goodness of people's hearts, or from the satisfaction of "making a contribution." Salaried and hourly employees alike may indeed take pride in doing better work and in having their opinions respected. But the paycheck, the company benefits package, job security, and the opportunity to earn a little something extra are also indispensable ingredients in employee involvement and loyalty. On these counts, too, Ford has made enormous improvements in recent years.

A big step forward came with the 1982 Ford-UAW contract, which introduced a profit-sharing plan for hourly employees. The plan, which took effect in 1983, awarded year-end cash bonuses to workers on the basis of corporate profits and the individual employee's length of service with the company. By 1986, Ford workers who qualified under the plan received bonuses averaging $2,100 per person. And in 1987, when Ford made greater profits than any other U.S. automaker, those bonuses shot up to an average of $3,700 per person — the largest hourly employee profit-sharing distribution ever made by an American corporation! By contrast, hourly workers at General Motors were paid *no* year-end bonuses for 1986 or 1987.

Other Ford labor contracts negotiated in 1984 and 1987 addressed employee concerns over and above wage rates, monetary benefits, and bonuses. The emphasis in these contracts was upon job security and company-sponsored employee education and training — including retraining and the development of new job skills for both active and laid-off employees. The meat-and-potatoes issues were already covered well for Ford's hourly work force, and the thrust of the company's employee relations was clearly centering more on the "human" considerations. Building a new corporate culture was a serious and well-articulated goal of the company. The 1987 annual report, in fact, contained a two-page spread under the title "Corporate Culture." This was the first time in the company's history that such a section appeared in the annual report.

At Ford, a calculated effort is being made to shape its culture into an environment that is more hospitable, stimulating, and rewarding for all of its members who are willing to play an active role. The betting is that such an environment will continue to stimulate those "better ideas" that set Ford apart.

6

Better Ideas
from Without

Securing greater employee involvement was indispensable
to the success of Team Taurus. But Ford management
also recognized — for the first time, to any serious degree — that
the company had important *outside* constituents who could
make useful contributions if approached in the right way.

There were, of course, the consumers, whose ideas and
wishes historically had been given little more than casual attention by American automakers. There were Ford's own dealers,
as well as fleet owners, car rental agencies, and automotive garages
and body shops. And then there was one group that, although
absolutely vital to the manufacturers, had traditionally been
treated like poor cousins. These were the thousands of parts suppliers and subcontractors who furnished the auto industry with
everything from nuts and bolts to sheet steel, carpeting, transmission chains, dipsticks, and complete headlight assemblies.

Ford, like other U.S. auto manufacturers, had always
"shopped" its suppliers, typically treating them as impersonal
sources that were to be haggled with or otherwise pressured into

delivering components at the lowest possible price and often under unreasonable schedules. In some cases, the relationship between automaker and parts supplier even bordered on being adversarial. At best, dealing with suppliers was usually a matter of "horse-trading," with sketchy communications and seldom any real sense of cooperation or long-term mutual benefit. The automaker's engineers drew up specifications for a component, and then the purchasing department sent around the spec sheets to a number of suppliers for bids. If a supplier was technically capable of making the component, the main consideration was price. Suppliers who came in with the lowest bids got the jobs.

It's easy to see that this system didn't inspire much concern about quality. In addition, automakers often contracted with more than one supplier to furnish the same component. This frequently led to a lack of uniformity in the quality, dimensions, or fit of a particular component across the whole line of cars being manufactured. Not every Mustang, for example, had the same quality of carpeting or the same door-locking reliability as the next Mustang, because the carpeting or the door locks might each have been made by two or more different suppliers.

In gearing up to create the Taurus, however, Ford decided to try a new approach — this time in its out-sourcing and supplier relations. Four years before the slated start of production on the new cars, the purchasing specialists on Team Taurus developed a list of the best suppliers for each component. "Best" was not to be primarily a matter of low price, although that isn't to say the company was throwing economy to the winds. Ford certainly didn't want to pay more than necessary for its components, but "necessary" was defined differently now than in the past. *Quality* was the most important determinant. And right after quality came *reliability* and *cooperation* on the part of the supplier. Ford wanted suppliers who were willing to make a long-term commitment and who would do whatever was necessary to ensure quality and dependability. If this meant sometimes paying a slightly higher price for a component than under the old "low-bid" system, then so be it. And in any case, the Taurus was a new entity containing many redesigned or new components for which there was no easy comparison. Ford, in fact, designed more than 4,000 completely new parts for the cars, including such things as whole starter systems, alternators, sun visors, and even the oil dipstick.

Plans were also underway at Ford to adopt a "just-in-time" parts delivery program. The just-in-time system is largely self-explanatory. Manufacturers coordinate their parts requirements with suppliers so that the parts arrive at the factory as they are needed and in just the right quantities. This makes it unnecessary for the manufacturer to store and manage large inventories of diverse parts. A just-in-time system frees up space that would otherwise be needed for storage, reduces the cost of shuffling parts around the factory, minimizes confusion in getting the right parts to the right place on time, and lessens the potential for damage to parts through repeated handling. Suppliers benefit by being able to smooth out their production schedules and thus avoid the highs and lows of intermittent massive production runs and slack times. In many cases, suppliers themselves can take advantage of just-in-time delivery on their own purchased components and raw materials.

While simple in concept, a just-in-time delivery system requires careful coordination and close communication between supplier and manufacturer. By its nature, it requires an ongoing relationship. The manufacturer doesn't simply place a one-time order for, say, 120,000 speedometer cables and then stockpile them in some warehouse adjacent to the assembly plant, waiting for installation in new cars over a twelve-month period. Instead, the order is apt to be for something like 10,000 cables delivered each month to meet the plant's just-in-time needs. With the continuing relationship that ensues, the manufacturer and supplier have more occasions to communicate with each other and better opportunities to spot problems as, or before, they come up.

This sort of relationship was exactly what Ford was looking for in its new approach to outside resources, although it wasn't solely for the sake of just-in-time delivery. "What we wanted," said Lewis Veraldi, "was for our suppliers to participate fully in the entire development process. We wanted them to understand what we were trying to accomplish and be able to react quickly with us in accommodating design changes all the way through the program."

To begin building such relationships, it made sense to start very early — even before design sketches of the Taurus were available to show to prospective suppliers. Of course, many of the companies that would eventually be chosen for the program had already been suppliers to Ford. But they were accustomed to the old wheeling-and-dealing process of securing one-shot contracts. Ford now had a new message and an unfamiliar proposition to put before them. Just as so many of Ford's "new" ideas at this time sprang from basic, simple common sense, so, too, did this one. "If you're willing to truly collaborate with us and give us an extraordinary effort," said Ford, "we're willing to concentrate our business with you and give you a long-term contract."

Altogether, about 400 outside suppliers were brought into the Taurus-Sable program on this basis from the very beginning. Ford signed individual long-term contracts ranging up to five years with most of these suppliers. By thus assuring the suppliers of continuing and fairly steady business, Ford gained a little extra leverage in insisting on high quality standards. The long-term commitment also encouraged and enabled suppliers to tailor their operations to Ford's needs. By becoming involved very early in the program, suppliers had longer lead times to work out improved production methods and quality-control systems.

Another important strategy in Ford's new sourcing program was the selection of single suppliers for each key component. For example, instead of buying various pieces of interior plastic trim from several different sources, Ford contracted with a single supplier for all interior plastic trim. With the greater volume ensured by such a contract, the supplier could afford to concentrate more of its resources on the job and would most likely be more quality-conscious. Furthermore, this tended to guarantee greater uniformity in the product. All of the interior plastic trim, for example, would be of the same color tone, surface grain, thickness, and so on. Most importantly, it would all be of the same dimensions and fit — thus minimizing the number of discarded parts, easing the job of assembly, and ensuring a better fit and finish in the car's interior.

Much like the Employee Involvement program, Ford's new approach to supplier relations was intended to tap the know-how and experience of people whose opinions had seldom if ever been given much credibility in Detroit. The company actively encouraged suppliers to contribute their ideas and criticisms, and before long, Ford executives began referring to selected suppliers as "members of Team Taurus." Preferred suppliers offered many concrete suggestions to enhance the quality of Ford's new cars, and even to improve manufacturing efficiency in the company's plants.

An automotive chain manufacturer, for example, helped Ford engineers design an exceptionally quiet transmission chain for the Taurus's new automatic overdrive transaxle.

Another supplier recommended and then helped design a retractable tailgate picnic table for the Taurus and Sable station wagons.

A carpet supplier pointed out that the carpeting in many station wagon cargo areas has a multicolored appearance simply because the carpet is installed in separate pieces, with the nap running haphazardly in different directions. Upon learning this, Ford specified that the Taurus and Sable station wagon carpets be aligned so that all the nap ran in the same direction, thus producing a smoother, more "finished" look.

Still another supplier proposed and helped develop Taurus's dual sun visor and pull-down visor vanity mirror. This same company redesigned the lenses on the interior reading lights to eliminate glare and reflections that could interfere with the driver's vision at night.

The success of the supplier program hasn't depended solely on the introduction of specific product improvements or inventive new processes. More important to its success was the fact that Ford asked for the suppliers' help — and then *listened* to their responses. The real gains — better communications, tighter coordination, the ability to react quickly and economically to changing requirements, and a steady advance in predictable levels of product quality — have been incremental and cumulative.

At one supplier company, a testing laboratory supervisor said he was impressed with Ford's new manufacturer-supplier teamwork philosophy because "usually the suppliers of components know more about those components than the automaker does itself." The president of another firm said, "Ford planned the Taurus about as well as it can be done, and it was especially important to bring in suppliers like us very early in the process."

As Ford's select list of outside suppliers evolved, the company devised a formal program to acknowledge the ones who performed with special distinction. The "Q-1 Preferred Quality Award" was created to honor these suppliers — but it was not to be an easy award to come by. Ford applies very rigorous standards in picking the honorees, and thus, becoming a "Q-1" supplier is a truly notable accomplishment. Like the EI program, it is not merely a superficial public relations gimmick.

Prospective recipients are evaluated by a team made up of Ford corporate-level product quality specialists, product engineers, and representatives of the individual Ford plants that are served by the supplier in question. Special attention is given to the quality of components and raw materials and to the supplier's systems and procedures for ongoing quality control. Heavy emphasis is also placed on the supplier's ability to react quickly and efficiently to changing requirements. A Q-1 supplier must be able to maintain a continuously high level of product quality while retooling or installing new manufacturing processes and statistical control methods.

The key goal is the *prevention* of quality breakdowns, rather than the discovery of defects after the fact. The Q-1 Award is Ford's way of extending to its preferred suppliers the same standard that it adopted for its own operations in 1980: defect prevention, rather than detection. For Ford, as well as its Q-1 suppliers, the successful application of this quality-control philosophy pays off in two important ways. It not only helps ensure the higher quality — and hence, better marketability — of the end-product; it also saves money by eliminating the need for much redundant testing, end-of-line inspections, repairs, double handling of the product, and scrappage of materials. Since Ford itself began concentrating on defect prevention, the company has been able to cut back greatly on its inspection staff and eliminate a large number of product reworking or repair stations in its plants. Many people who used to work as inspectors and repair specialists have now been reassigned to *production* jobs.

The Ford and Mercury dealers who were to sell the Taurus and the Sable were obviously critical outside resources as well. Ford might be able to manufacture great cars, and the corporate promotion staff and outside advertising agencies might be able to favorably precondition the market, but the dealers and their salespeople form the final link with the customer.

As important as this link is — and always has been — American automakers have traditionally taken the dealers pretty much for granted. Dealer-level sales training support from Detroit has always been rather superficial, and even the essentials of product knowledge have usually been shortchanged. Cars and trucks still get sold, of course — because people need them. Brand loyalty or the persuasive effects of national advertising can also take the sale away from the competition, even when the salesperson is poorly informed or otherwise ineffectual. But by and large, Detroit still has a long way to go in strengthening the final link with its customers.

The nation's fifth largest car and truck dealership — a Ford dealer with 1987 sales of more than $128 million — told the authors that one of the biggest obstacles to selling *twice* as many vehicles as he does is a lack of product knowledge and sales training support for his selling staff, knowledge and training that he feels can come only from the manufacturer. This dealer did acknowledge a substantial improvement in such support from Ford where the Taurus is concerned, but he felt that help is needed in the many other product lines. A salesperson, he explained, can easily get confused and discouraged because there's so much to know about so many different products. "You've got half a dozen different car models and just as many trucks and vans," he said, "and all of them have different packages of features, options, and price-points. It's really just too much for most people to carry all of this around in their heads, especially when they're demonstrating one product one minute and a completely different one ten or fifteen minutes later. Something has to be done to simplify this knowledge and train these people better on a continuing basis."

Actually, this dealer's complaint may reflect something that is simply endemic to today's car business. Detroit has always offered a smorgasbord of models and variations on models, targeting virtually every customer niche that consumer researchers and demographers have been able to identify. And regardless of the attrition of U.S. carmakers, the import invasion has contributed to the proliferation of automotive products. The result at the retail level is confusion — for car buyers and car sellers alike. It exists not merely among different brands and different dealers but *within* any given dealership selling the many models and variations of the same nameplate.

One obvious solution is to limit the choices — produce fewer models and reduce the variety of packages and options. Ford, in fact, has begun to use this strategy by reducing what it calls "marketing entity complexity." More features that used to be considered add-ons or options for a Taurus-class car have now been made standard. The result is that the Taurus (and Sable) salesperson has fewer versions of the cars to explain to prospective customers.

Ford knew, however, that this wasn't enough; it had to do a better job of preparing its dealers to sell the Taurus and Sable. The targeted customers for the vehicles were profiled as generally above-average in education, fairly knowledgeable about what they wanted in a car, and somewhat more discriminating than the average buyer about style, quality, and value-for-money. It was important, then, that Taurus and Sable salespeople be given more than the typical product knowledge and sales training. This was even more critical considering the radical new styling of the cars and their decidedly superior quality — *both* of which were uncommon features for an American car at that time.

Ford dealers were accustomed to receiving a standard kit of product information and recommended selling points for each new car only a short time before the car's market introduction.

This kit normally consisted of a "facts book" and videotape cassettes describing the car's physical features and outlining its performance benefits. It also included slick, four-color promotional brochures designed primarily for customers. With the Taurus and Sable, however, Ford went a couple of steps further and started the dealer education process much earlier.

Several months before the planned introduction of the cars, separate manuals for each vehicle were specially prepared and circulated to the dealerships, detailing the revolutionary concepts embodied in the cars, such as the ergonomical design, and explaining the practical benefits of the new aerodynamic body style. The company also bombarded the dealerships with newsletters reporting on progress in the development program and explaining new or upgraded features of the cars. This helped maintain a continuing awareness and heightened expectation among dealers and their sales personnel.

Most importantly, Ford made sure that its dealers got as early an exposure as possible to the cars themselves. Ordinarily, a dealer salesperson's first hands-on involvement with a new model comes through test-driving a "demonstrator" from the first shipment of the cars to the dealership. But with the Taurus and Sable, the company made working prototypes of the cars available to dealers well in advance of the market release date for what was called a "ride-and-drive experience." Ford personnel who were thoroughly familiar with the cars rode with dealer salespeople and explained the vehicles' unique quality features, performance characteristics, and competitive edge over other nameplates in the same class. Through this advance personal exposure to the cars, Ford hoped to build an unusual degree of anticipation and enthusiasm among the dealers long before the cars were ready for the showroom floors.

To stimulate a greater team identity among its dealers, Ford has also created a special dealership award program. Called the "President's Award," it is a highly select recognition of outstanding dealer performance. And like the Q-1 Award for suppliers, it is not handed out casually. To earn the President's Award, a Ford or Lincoln-Mercury dealer must score exceptionally high on customer surveys conducted routinely by the company. The criteria are based on overall customer satisfaction with the dealership, including the courtesy, competence, and helpfulness of salespeople, the ease and simplicity of concluding a purchase, the quality of preparation on the car prior to customer delivery, and the convenience and reliability of follow-up maintenance and repair service. The exacting criteria for being selected are illustrated by the fact that only 119 of 5,600 Ford and Lincoln-Mercury dealers won the award in 1987. In addition, there is significant prestige in an award that is personally presented, not by some regional representative or middle-level manager, but by the highest ranking executives of the Ford Motor Company — usually the president or the vice chairman. The award presentations are also made with great fanfare at a select vacation resort site.

Consulting outside resources steadily became an article of faith at Ford during the early 1980s. The company's key suppliers became involved as never before; the dealers were brought onto the team; and consultants such as W. Edwards Deming were asked for their expert advice. But there were still other outsiders who had contributions to make.

For example, Ford surveyed auto body repair shops for help in pinpointing areas where the new cars might be especially vulnerable to serious collision damage and therefore excessively difficult or expensive to fix. As a result of these surveys, the company identified previously overlooked trouble spots that could be reengineered for greater safety and more economical collision repairs. The studies also led to the development of a comprehensive collision repair manual for the Taurus and Sable — the first specialized publication of its type produced by an American automaker and offered to dealers and repair shops.

As mentioned elsewhere, no American new-car program had ever been subjected to such long and intense consumer research. For more than five years, and at an unprecedented cost, Ford sought the opinions, criticisms, and advice of American drivers on virtually every aspect of the new cars' development. Even before preliminary design sketches were made for the cars, Ford was surveying consumer opinion on front-wheel drive. Three and a half years before job one, the company was showing consumers photographs of clay models; six months later, consumers were viewing interior and exterior fiberglass mock-ups of the cars; and three years away from production, surveys were being conducted on prospective names.

Styling clinics were held as early as 1981, and in 1984 full ride-and-drive clinics were conducted using actual production-representative prototypes. By the time the Taurus and Sable went to market in December 1985, they had been pretested more than any other cars in U.S. automotive history. Several thousand consumers and media representatives had already driven or ridden in them, and thousands more had at least seen the cars and had responded to research questions about them.

One consumer test-driving program conducted by Ford in collaboration with Hertz Rent-a-Car permitted some 4,000 people to try out the cars about six months before they were released. Ford selected prominent figures and opinion-leaders in six test markets — Los Angeles, San Francisco, Chicago, Denver, New York, and Atlanta — and distributed 500 preproduction models of the Taurus and Sable to Hertz outlets in those markets. Ford vice presidents then sent personal letters to the selected consumers, inviting them to contact Hertz for the free use of a car for two to three days. Hertz delivered the cars fully fueled and ready to drive, then picked them up, cleaned and refueled them, and delivered them to the next test-driver. All of the drivers were guaranteed that they would *not* receive any follow-up contacts from Ford dealers. They were asked only to try out the cars and complete a questionnaire about the experience. A few were also invited to take part in focus-group research sessions.

This program was a revolutionary departure from Detroit's typical kind of research. But it represented what was by then becoming the norm at Ford: looking to the outside, as well as the inside, for ideas and answers.

Throughout the program, consumers provided many useful suggestions. Some of them, for example, complained that most cars had inadequate foot room for rear-seat passengers. They said that they had to stick their feet under the back of the front seat, and when they did, they often scuffed their shoes on the metal seat-adjustment tracks. Ford solved this problem by sloping the floor beneath the front seats, widening the space between the adjustment tracks, and making the tracks of smooth plastic instead of metal.

Other consumers reminded Ford that this is the "do-it-yourself" age, when more drivers than ever before perform routine service on their own cars. Indeed, with full-service gas stations fast disappearing from the nation's roads and streets, drivers are increasingly forced to check the oil and coolant levels, change or top off the oil, refill windshield-washer reservoirs, and inspect hoses, filters, and fan belts. Recognizing this, Ford designed the Taurus and Sable engine compartments to provide easy access to these components. Taking it a step further, the company color-coded all such components in yellow and attached a plastic servicing information plaque within easy view at the front of the engine. The servicing instructions on this plaque were written in both English and Spanish to reflect the changing composition of American society.

It was this kind of out-sourcing for ideas that, in the end, set the Taurus and Sable apart from the competition. As Philip Caldwell, and later Donald Petersen, had mandated, Team Taurus *listened*. Ford's listening to all these people, however, involved a delicate balancing act. As noted earlier, not everything the customers contributed would necessarily be valid, realistically achievable, or consistent with the integrated totality of the car. Likewise, some of the suggestions from dealers, suppliers, or employees might be irrelevant or unproductive. The challenge was to stay on target with the main mission of building an all-round superior car — while trying, wherever possible, to incorporate the best of the new ideas that everybody now seemed so willing to offer.

7

On the
Road Again

Between the end of 1979 and the beginning of 1985, the Ford Motor Company had already broken so many Detroit traditions that it hardly resembled an American automaking firm any longer. Of course, the general public wasn't aware of the many changes occurring in the company, but people were going to learn a lot about the "new Ford" in 1985 and 1986.

In earlier chapters, we've noted that the aerodynamic styling of the Taurus was a calculated risk, considering the typically conservative mind-set and tastes of the mid-market segment at which the car was aimed. We've also seen that Ford began easing the new aero look into the American public eye in 1983 with the Thunderbird, Cougar, Tempo, Topaz, and Lincoln Mark VII. The Thunderbird and Cougar, however, are classified as specialty cars, and as such, they could be more daring in style. The Lincoln Mark VII, aimed at an upscale luxury market, could also afford to be somewhat different because its targeted customers tend to be a bit more worldly and receptive to new ideas, especially if those new ideas carry an international flavor. And the modern aerostyling trend in cars was associated at that time with European names like Mercedes-Benz and Audi.

But Ford was naturally concerned about the *mass* market, where big-volume sales were at stake. That's where the Tempo and Topaz compacts played a very important role in helping to condition the public for what was to come later. The 1983-84 Tempo and Topaz were aerodynamically styled, but not nearly to the degree that was planned for the Taurus and Sable. After a somewhat slow beginning, the Tempo and Topaz gained popularity and enjoyed sales success in the moderately priced compact sedan segment. This demonstrated to Ford that at least a certain level of aerostyling was acceptable in the mass market.

In a 1987 report, L. R. Windecker, Ford's research and analysis manager, wrote:

> The 1984 sales success of the compact-sized, moderate-priced aerodynamic Topaz and Tempo sedans was greeted with quiet relief at Ford, as the somewhat larger and upscale Taurus and Sable sedans and wagons, to be introduced in 1985, were already off the drawing boards, through the prototype shops, and running on Ford's test tracks and proving grounds. Ford had crossed the mass-market Rubicon with Tempo and Topaz — there was no turning back.

At about the same time, Louis Lataif, then vice president for NAAO sales operations, declared, "Tempo and Topaz led the way for Ford in opening the mass automotive market to the concept of aerodynamic styling. The success of Taurus and Sable rests firmly on the pioneering market forays of Tempo and Topaz."

Windecker and Lataif, of course, were speaking retrospectively in 1987. At the beginning of 1985, however, when it was committed irrevocably to the Taurus and Sable and was facing the imminent start-up of production on the cars, Ford was *still* nervous about the styling. The Taurus and Sable, after all, would carry the aerodynamic look well beyond that of their predecessors, and the cars still had to win the affections of the mid-market.

An internal market research memorandum circulated in late 1984 told of "danger signals concerning the public perception of Ford's new aerodynamic look." The memo concluded that these research findings called for "pre-introduction communications and product exposure actions." In other words, it was show-and-tell time, and Ford had a lot more showing and telling to do. The successes of the Tempo and Topaz notwithstanding, further education and persuasion were needed to precondition the market before the Taurus and Sable were released — especially if the cars were to achieve management's ambitious goal of appealing to six out of ten car-buyers in their market segments.

The situation clearly called for the company's public relations experts to make an extraordinary effort. Of course, the public relations people had already been doing their job. Ford's public affairs department, headed by David W. Scott, had been working on the pre-launch program for several months in anticipation of the originally planned April 1985 release date for the cars. But it was getting rather late in the game to discover that there was still a consumer perception problem with so basic an issue as the aerostyling.

As it turned out, however, the release date for the Taurus and Sable was postponed, primarily to correct some computer software problems in the assembly plants, but also to make some improvements on the cars themselves. Ford was taking its ongoing consumer research very seriously, and if there had to be a delay because of factory problems, then the extra time could also be used to answer some consumer preferences and complaints that the research was turning up.

Ford, like the other auto firms, had always tried to adhere strictly to all scheduled dates for job one and product launch. It was almost a matter of religion in Detroit. Once a date had been set and announced, it was virtually sacred. As David Scott puts it, "Careers used to rest on meeting job one and new-product introduction dates." But Ford was forced to break the rule because too much was at stake. These cars *had* to be right, and the production lines had to be ready to run without crashing.

In the end, the release date was delayed even beyond the first postponement, and Ford took some flak over it from the trade press and competitors. Some people interpreted the successive delays as evidence that Ford was in even more serious trouble than was previously thought.

On the bright side, however, was the extra time given to Scott's group and the marketing people to broaden and improve the public's perception of the cars. Almost a full year was now available to carry out the market education and promotion program. And Scott's group, with the help of others, used that year to the fullest possible advantage.

The twelve-month-long launch program for Taurus was not only the longest in American automotive history but also the most diverse and imaginative. The credit for this goes to the North American public affairs team. David Scott told the members of the team, in effect, to pull out all the stops. It was no time to be conservative, or even discreet.

The first major event carried out by the launch team was unique not only in its character but also in its timing. On January 29, 1985, eleven months before the Taurus and Sable would actually reach the market, Ford staged a splashy Hollywood preview of the cars. The unveiling of a new car model so far in advance of its market release was unprecedented. Furthermore, the annual Chicago auto show was to be held only ten days later, and there were people who wondered why Ford chose to stage its own preview in Hollywood first. The Chicago show was traditionally the biggest automotive exposition in the country and was expected to draw more than a million visitors. Of course, Ford also took the Taurus and Sable to the Chicago show, but the company wanted its exclusive Hollywood extravaganza for good reasons.

As we've noted earlier, California is the nation's trend-setter in new consumer products, especially where new or unusual styling is concerned. Ford officials felt that by showing the cars first in California, they were more likely to get an initial burst of enthusiasm, which they hoped would carry over to later previews and additional auto shows. The major media would all be at the

Hollywood event, and their anticipated approval of the cars might be infectious throughout the country. Besides, media representatives from places like Detroit, Philadelphia, and Milwaukee were apt to be in a more receptive mood simply because of the glamorous surroundings and the California weather.

In addition, the very idea of previewing a new car in California was unique — and the way in which it was orchestrated was in the best Hollywood tradition. The company booked a soundstage at the MGM studios and performed an unveiling of the cars that smacked of pure show business glitz. The soundstage was the one that had been used for filming parts of "Gone with the Wind," and more recently for the science-fiction movie "War Games." Some of the props from "War Games" were still in place, a fact that Ford hoped would complement the somewhat futuristic personality of the new cars.

A full day of activities was planned for the select group of invited guests. Among them were various Hollywood celebrities, as well as a large corps of mass media and trade press representatives. Reporters, columnists, editors, and broadcasters from 370 news and business press organizations were invited. Major portions of the day's program were broadcast live over Ford's own satellite-aided Employee Communications Network, reaching thousands of the company's employees throughout the country. Video coverage was also provided by satellite to commercial television stations nationwide.

In addition to the MGM studios, Ford used three prestigious Los Angeles-area hotels for the gala — the Beverly Wilshire, the Bel Air, and the Century Plaza. Technical exhibits were set up in conference rooms, displaying the cars' many new features and allowing guests to see how they were designed and engineered. A formal press conference was held early in the day, and Ford engineers, designers, and other specialists were later made available to the media for informal interviews on technical matters.

Among the key executives participating in these interviews were Jack Telnack and Lewis Veraldi. But even more significant was the fact that Ford also brought along its highest echelon of management — a move calculated to dramatize the commitment that the corporation had made to these two new cars. Chairman Philip Caldwell and President Donald Petersen led the entourage. Also on hand was Harold Poling, who was then executive vice president of NAAO and was soon to become president and chief operating officer of Ford. In a brief speech, Poling summed up Ford's posture on this momentous occasion. "Our quality is up, our profits are up, our costs are down, and we're in good fighting shape."

The official unveiling — or, as Ford called it, the "premiere" — of the new cars was held at the end of the day, following a reception and dinner presided over by Caldwell and Petersen. Once the guests had been given ample time to inspect and admire the cars, the whole event was concluded by an hour-long session that was billed on the agenda as the "afterglow."

Judging from the response of the media, the Tinseltown bash was indeed a glowing success. *USA Today* wrote: "The Hollywood setting for [Ford's] preview is appropriate. In recent years, Ford has staged the kind of turnaround that usually happens only in movies."

In a written critique five days after the event, Ford's David Scott reported that the media gave "nothing but outstanding reviews on the program." Of course, the real issue wasn't whether the guests had enjoyed themselves, but what did they think of the new cars? That, too, would be answered quite positively, from Ford's viewpoint, in the coming weeks and months as the trade and mass media published and broadcast story after story extolling the Taurus and congratulating the Ford Motor Company on its turnaround. Many reporters and editors portrayed the cars as being on the leading edge of auto technology, driving performance, and design efficiency. Some media saw the Taurus-Sable program as evidence of Ford's "comeback," and others described the aerodynamic styling as a "gamble won." *Fortune* magazine later ran an issue featuring Taurus in a cover story. Donald Petersen appeared on the *Fortune* cover, half kneeling in front of a new Taurus. Other key magazine feature stories appeared in *Forbes* and the *New York Times Sunday Magazine*.

Of course, the heavy and overwhelmingly positive media coverage that the Taurus was to enjoy over the coming twelve months didn't all spring from the Hollywood preview. But that event nonetheless set the tone for the rest of Ford's publicity campaign and perhaps sowed the seeds of enthusiasm among media people. The Taurus was good enough in its own right to deserve the media accolades it was to get, but its show biz debut probably gave the promotion effort an earlier and livelier impetus than might have occurred with a more prosaic introduction.

In the week following the Hollywood event, Ford took the Taurus and Sable to the Chicago Auto Show, where the cars were revealed for the first time to the general public. As mentioned earlier, working prototypes of the cars had been shown to and even driven by various groups of consumers for research purposes on other occasions, but in Chicago the cars would be seen for the first time by a mass audience of consumers. On the evening before the official opening of the show, Ford's public affairs department held a news conference attended by all of the primary Chicago media, as well as by several Detroit and Canadian publications and broadcast organizations. The Chicago bureaus of national and international wire services also sent representatives, and coverage was given by Chicago's network television stations, as well as by WGN-TV, the Windy City's "super station" that is linked to more than forty states via cable. One important piece of nationwide publicity that came out of this press conference was an interview with Ford executives appearing on Dan Rather's CBS evening news show.

Ford got some additional mileage from the Chicago Auto Show by revealing that its Chicago assembly plant would be the second facility to produce the Taurus and Sable. This, obviously, attracted some special attention from the local media.

During the twelve-month publicity blitz that was kicked off in Hollywood, Ford hosted media events involving more than 1,500 general news and trade press representatives. Some 350 of these writers, editors, and broadcasters were also given the chance to test-drive the new cars. The scale, intensity, and degree of hands-on exposure in this media promotion program were quite unusual, if not virtually unique, for Detroit. A certain amount of hoopla had always accompanied the introduction of a new car model, but the Taurus was paraded before the media and the public as no car had ever been so far in advance of its actual market release.

Furthermore, as late as February 1985 — following the public previewing of the Taurus and Sable in Chicago — Ford was still conducting consumer tests on the vehicles. This was partly for the purpose of actual research, which the company would continue doing right up to the moment for job one, when the first of the new cars started down the assembly line. Indeed, research would go on even beyond that point. But another reason for the continuing consumer tests was to provide further exposure of the cars' aerostyling to ordinary consumers, as well as to selected "opinion leaders" in different communities around the country.

In late February 1985, for example, Ford asked 160 new-car buyers and four journalists in Boca Raton, Florida, to perform comparison driving tests of the Taurus LX sedan and a disguised model of the Chevrolet Celebrity CL sedan. The participants were asked to do the same with a Sable LS station wagon and an Oldsmobile Cutlass Ciera Cruiser station wagon. The consumers were each paid $50 to participate.

Even at this late date, the company was still looking for consumer reactions to cars that were already designed, engineered, and just about ready to go into production. But it was also hoping that for every driver who tried — and liked — the cars, there would be some favorable word-of-mouth publicity that could precondition any number of other potential customers. Each Boca Raton test-driver who liked the Taurus or the Sable might tell one, two, or a dozen friends about the car, and this kind of pre-release "grapevine" promotion could nicely complement all of the professional media publicity.

Ford's stated research purpose for the Boca Raton tests was "to determine customer acceptance of Taurus and Sable features, package, ergonomics, styling, ride, handling, and performance, as well as to identify any particular dislikes." A company report on the program called the tests "a good learning experience." And as a result of this learning, the company did, in fact, make some changes on the cars prior to job one in Atlanta six months later.

In every important respect, the consumers and journalists who took part in the Boca Raton tests were very favorably impressed with the Taurus and Sable. Only two complaints emerged that justified small changes. Some of the test subjects felt the cars' acceleration from a dead stop wasn't quite as good as the Celebrity's. Ford officials later pointed out that Taurus and Sable acceleration was actually better than that of the Celebrity from zero to sixty miles per hour, but they nonetheless made a minor adjustment to "soup up" the start in the lower speed range. The second complaint had to do with a hood latch that was somewhat hard to operate and that scratched people's fingers. Ford solved the problem by replacing the metal latch with a smooth plastic piece.

Other hands-on promotion efforts that came as much as a full year ahead of the cars' market introduction included events like an automotive trade press preview at Fords' Design Center. This session was held in early 1985 and was attended by eleven key automotive writers. Nine of these writers were staff members of individual magazines, and two were freelancers who wrote regularly for twenty-five other publications. All of these were "long-lead" publications that require several months of lead time for publication deadlines. In addition to the strictly automotive-oriented media were such magazines as *Consumer Reports, Town and Country, Popular Science, Popular Mechanics,* and *Mechanix Illustrated.*

Later in 1985, Ford hosted representatives of 77 national and big-city news media at the Dearborn Center and allowed them to drive prototypes of the Taurus and Sable. After that, 60 production models of the cars were taken around the country for test-driving by local journalists in 100 medium-size and small cities and towns. Ford's early, heavy, and persistent attention to the media went far beyond the norm for Detroit at that time.

Of all the pre-release promotion activities Ford conducted throughout 1985, the Hollywood unveiling certainly ranked as a unique and creative event. But even more unusual was another program carried out by Charles Gumushian of the North American public affairs team.

Team Taurus and Ford corporate officials knew that it was absolutely essential to get as many people as possible *personally* involved with the cars before they reached the market. Out of this necessity came the invention of a remarkable program — the "caravan." It was really a quite simple idea, but like so many of Ford's ideas by this time, it represented an unheard-of departure from Detroit's stodgy ways.

It should be recalled that two of Ford's most important new strategies were the involvement of employees and closer relations with suppliers. The caravan was designed to reinforce these strategies and to get local media coverage in the towns and cities visited. In March 1985, working prototypes of the Taurus and Sable were loaded onto two moving vans and hauled around the country for live showings at Ford facilities and supplier plants. In addition to the cars themselves, the caravan carried technical exhibits displaying some of the advanced components and systems designed for the new vehicles. Team Taurus members accompanied the caravan to meet with community leaders, to help present the cars to company and supplier personnel, and to conduct interviews with local news media.

One very important aspect of this caravan tour was that it took the cars into many small, out-of-the-way communities where automotive news was seldom featured in local papers or on local television. It was the first truly "grass-roots" publicity effort ever undertaken so far in advance of a new car's release by a Detroit automaker. New York City, Atlanta, Chicago, and Detroit are all accustomed to being the focus of attention and to being courted by national-scale interests. But many places where the caravan visited — such as Connersville, Indiana; Spartanburg, South Carolina; Huntsville, Alabama; and Carlisle, Pennsylvania — rarely find themselves in the spotlight.

Ford's announced mission for the caravan was to thank its suppliers and its employees in outlying plants for their contributions in creating the Taurus. The company wanted to show workers and plant managers how their specific jobs had fit into the whole picture and hoped to encourage them to take a sense of pride in what they had accomplished. One of the stock comments by Ford officials on the caravan was, "We want to show you the results of your work. These are *your* cars because, without you, they couldn't have been built."

This certainly was an admirable gesture — and it worked beautifully. Everywhere the caravan stopped, local Ford employees and supplier personnel were, on the whole, very impressed with the cars and pleased that Ford was making the effort to thank them and include them on the Taurus team.

"I think it's the best thing Ford ever did," said a millwright at a small-town Ford plant. "It's a good little front-wheel-drive car that will take the market. *I'm* going to buy one."

"The style and overall balance of design are very impressive," said another production worker. "The designers have taken everything into consideration."

"It's nice to see what our efforts are going to," explained a testing-lab supervisor at a supplier plant. "We appreciate the team approach that Ford took with the Taurus."

A supplier executive said, "It's been fun for our workers because it's given them a sense of involvement they haven't felt before."

There were literally thousands of such responses from company and supplier personnel throughout the caravan tour.

One woman, a thirty-five-year veteran employee with an automotive carpet supplier, said she had often wondered "what in the world they do with all the carpet we make." After inspecting the new Taurus station wagon and commenting on its roominess, she added, "I can see now that they find a place for it."

Many other workers described the Taurus and Sable as simply the "best," the "nicest," or the "greatest" cars Ford ever built. Many also expressed their appreciation of the caravan itself. This couldn't help but further boost the already improving relations between management and employees, and between Ford and its preferred suppliers.

Just as important for the company, however, was the grassroots media publicity generated by the caravan. With small-town as well as big-city papers and television stations reporting on the caravan, Ford was gaining incalculable amounts of free advertising. It's impossible to estimate how many people this publicity reached or how many it affected favorably, but there's no doubt that it greatly served Ford's objective of pre-conditioning the marketplace for its new look.

The original caravan, which ran from March to May, was so successful that a second one was organized for August to November of 1985. Overall, the two caravans reached 110 Ford and supplier plants in 100 U.S. and Canadian cities and towns and directly exposed the new cars to more than half a million company and supplier employees. Untold millions of other people learned of the cars and saw pictures of them in local newspapers and on local television. The caravan technique, in fact, paid such great dividends with the Taurus and Sable that Ford used it again for the pre-release promotion of its 1988 Lincoln Continental sedan. The same two vans that carried the Taurus and Sable around the country were overhauled and repainted for the Lincoln tour in late 1987.

As if Ford had not broken enough of Detroit's time-worn rules, the company had yet another surprise in store. As mentioned earlier, start-up production on the Taurus and Sable was delayed because of technical problems in manufacturing and because of management's decision to add some last-minute improvements to the cars. As Lewis Veraldi put it, "There was too much at stake to hurry things after we'd gotten this far. We delayed production a number of months because we wanted to ensure that everything would be just right."

By mid-1985, it was obvious that the cars wouldn't be ready for the dealers' showrooms until sometime during the winter. The question then became: Do we wait until after the start of the new year? If the cars were to go on the market in November or early December, Ford would be competing for the public's attention amid the cacophony of Christmas advertising. That was unacceptable, but so, too, was the idea of releasing 1986-model cars *in 1986*. Perhaps this was one industry tradition that shouldn't be totally scrapped by Ford.

The decision was then made to do something that to many observers might have seemed bizarre. December 26 was chosen as the official release date. That, of course, was the day after Christmas, and more than a few people thought the idea was crazy. But there is always a touch of shrewdness in insanity, and Ford, while it might have seemed to be going mad, was getting shrewder all the time.

So, December 26 it was. The new cars were undraped in dealer showrooms from coast to coast the day after Christmas — and the response by the public and the media was immensely favorable.

Americans are supposed to suffer from a psychological syndrome called the "post-Christmas blahs" — or the emotional letdown after all the excitement, anticipation, and tension of the holiday season. This malady usually lasts for a few weeks following Christmas, and if Ford had waited another week or two to introduce the new cars, perhaps it would have found a gloomy, unresponsive consumer market. Most people, however, were undoubtedly still emotionally "up" on December 26. The afterglow of Christmas was still with them, and the bills hadn't come in yet. Equally (or more) important was the fact that the first few days and weeks after Christmas are a slow advertising period, especially for big-ticket items and for national television. Of course, there are always many post-holiday sales advertised locally to help the stores get rid of unsold gift merchandise. But, essentially, Ford had less competition in the media, both editorially and commercially, during the immediate post-holiday period. And the company took full advantage of this opportunity by staging an all-out advertising and publicity blitz.

Ford's year-long launch program for the Taurus and Sable achieved just about everything the company wanted it to achieve. The two cars had gotten extensive exposure in the trade press and in much of the general news media. A month after the cars went on the market, *Motor Trend* magazine said, "In a strange sense, we've known the Taurus for a long time. We've watched it take shape and grow up from an engineering mule [an early working version of a new car model] to finished product."

At the start of the public relations program, David Scott had announced the goal of having 50 percent of the American public aware of the Taurus by the time the car went on the market. It was an ambitious goal that, in the end, wouldn't quite be reached. But the program was nonetheless a great success. Ford's marketing research group began conducting "awareness" studies in July 1985, more than six months after the kick-off of the promotion program. The first study showed that only 12 percent of American car owners were aware of the Taurus, and that 15 percent were aware of the Sable. By October, however, Taurus awareness had jumped to 27 percent, and Sable's to 24 percent. Finally, just before the nationally advertised December 26 introduction of the cars, Taurus awareness was up to 35 percent, and Sable's was holding steady in the low twenties. Public awareness of the Taurus had tripled between July and December, and at the time of market release, one out of every three American drivers was aware of the car.

Millions of Americans, not just in the big cities but in small towns and rural areas as well, had read about the Taurus and Sable in their local papers and national magazines, had seen pre-production models of the cars with their own eyes, or had at least viewed pictures of them. In addition, thousands of Ford's own employees and supplier personnel around the country had received a morale-building experience through the caravan tours. There was a growing excitement throughout the Ford Motor Company. Industry observers knew, and many ordinary citizens sensed, that Ford was indeed back in the "better idea" business. There was to be a Ford in a lot of people's futures after all — and a futuristic Ford, at that.

Probably the most significant measure of the launch program's success was the fact that prior to the December 26 market introduction, Ford had already written more than 146,000 dealer orders — worth some $1.5 billion — for the Taurus and Sable; and over 20,000 of those were actual customer orders. The Taurus accounted for 130,000 advance dealer orders, and within the first quarter after its market release, the car had sold an actual total of 170,000 units. In fact, the combined total of advance orders and first-quarter sales exhausted the entire planned production of the car for the first two quarters of the year. Furthermore, it nearly exhausted the planned production for the first three quarters. Ford had projected "only" 195,000 sales through September, but 170,000 of those sales had been tallied by the end of March.

Other than Ford's competitors and perhaps a few cynics, about the only people who frowned on the massive and imaginative launch program were some of the company's own dealers and the people responsible for sales in the Ford and Lincoln-Mercury divisions. In late 1985 they still had 1985 vehicles to sell, and the advance Taurus and Sable orders generated by all the hoopla were undercutting their ability to move those inventories. Naturally, this problem can and does occur in varying degrees with almost all new model introductions. But with the Taurus program it was more dramatic because the launch itself was extraordinarily dramatic.

The role of the trade press and mass media, both before and after the Taurus-Sable introduction, was clearly a powerful factor in the initial success of the two cars. One can reasonably assume that the American media were hungry for a home-front automotive victory and were thus eager to jump on the bandwagon for anything legitimately promising that came out of Detroit. But the Taurus, as well as Ford's new ways of doing business, stood on their own merits.

In October 1985, *Car and Driver* had gotten enough of an advance look at the cars to become convinced. The magazine wrote: "The temptation at this point is for us to jump up and down and holler, 'Hey look at this.' The Taurus is as new as anything ever gets in Detroit. It's a milestone car that lives up to its billing." *Car and Driver* added: "The Taurus proves that, in America, Ford alone understands the automobile as a whole."

There were many such rave reviews in magazines and newspapers. According to *Road and Track*, "What Ford has accomplished here will make many a rival wish for another trip to the drawing board." And from *Popular Mechanics*: "After several hours of driving, we knew that Ford had done its homework on the Taurus."

Probably the most cherished and profitable accolade came from *Consumer Reports* in June 1986: "Overall, it scored the highest of any domestic car we've ever tested." For *Consumer Reports*, that was virtually the equivalent of a standing ovation.

In January 1986, the month following the public release of the cars, *Motor Trend* named the Taurus "Car of the Year" in North America — the most prestigious award that an American auto can win domestically. Close behind in second place was the Sable, and together the two cars, in the words of *Motor Trend*, "ran away from the rest of the competition."

Later that year, *Car and Driver* placed the Taurus and Sable in a tie for number one on its list of the ten best cars sold in the United States, and it ranked Ford's Lincoln Mark VII LSC third. Altogether, only four American-made cars were placed in the top-ten (in this case, top-eleven) list — and three of them were Ford products. The only other U.S. car to make it was the Chevrolet Corvette, which ranked fourth. In announcing its top-ten list, *Car and Driver* wrote: "We were starting to wonder if America would ever get up the gumption to build cars like the Taurus: friendly to look at, functional to use. Not only did Ford take the risk, it also spent the time and trouble to make its breakthrough sedans roadworthy and fun to drive. The American-made automobile will never be the same."

At the close of 1986, Taurus had become the best-selling mid-size car in the United States. It was also Ford's most dramatically successful new-model launch since the 1964 Mustang. A twenty-year drought at Ford had ended in a star-shower from the zodiac.

The caravan that was part of the strategy of preselling the Taurus was not only an effective public relations gambit, but it also symbolized Ford's new attitude toward its markets. The company was now getting out and around in the country in a way that neither it nor any other Detroit automaker had ever done before. Like the troubadour whose song was emanating from radios and jukeboxes throughout America about this time, the Ford Motor Company was "on the road again."

8

Winning
the World Over

Ford's extraordinary performance from 1986 onward does not, of course, guarantee an untroubled future or permanent prosperity. Some of the company's competitors and a few industry observers have continued to view Ford's new products and spectacular financial recovery as only transitory victories. Some have also argued that the company's successes have been more attributable to GM's troubles than to Ford's genius. Philip Caldwell himself said in mid-1988, "I never in my wildest dreams could have foreseen how badly GM has stumbled."

Just how badly is reflected in GM's loss of domestic auto share from 1978 through 1987 — down from 48 percent to 37.2 percent. A good portion of that loss was given up to the imports until Ford began making real inroads in the mid and late 1980s. After plunging to 16.6 percent in 1981, Ford's share of the domestic car market gradually climbed to 18.2 percent in 1986 and then jumped two percentage points to 20.2 percent in 1987. Ford grabbed another 1.7 points in the first six months of 1988, giving it a 21.9 percent share of the U.S. car market. After the devaluation of the U.S. dollar against the Japanese yen — which sent the price of Japanese cars soaring in the United States — it appeared that GM's chief concern over the next few years would not be the imports, but rather a Ford Motor Company that just keeps getting stronger.

General Motors is too big and too powerful to sit on its haunches and not put up a fight. By 1987, it was beginning to adopt some of the more innovative and successful aspects of the Taurus-Sable development, including the "Best-in-Class" concept, which the company calls its "Mona Lisa" program. GM has also picked up on the aerostyling theme; in fact, some of its recent television commercials seem to suggest that the very concept of aerodynamics was a GM discovery.

Then, of course, there's the highly publicized and rumor-plagued Saturn project, which, at a cost of some $4 billion, is expected to produce a totally new flagship car for GM. After six years in development, the first Saturn car is planned for introduction in the summer of 1990. GM has been secretive about the car itself, but industry analysts and media people have gleaned bits and pieces of intelligence that indicate the car will have an aluminum engine, a plastic gas tank, and — except for the hood and roof — an all-plastic body. Touted as a true breakthrough in automotive design, engineering, and production, the Saturn project appears to represent for GM what the Taurus-Sable program meant to Ford.

Thus, with its enormous financial strength and its fully modernized, highly automated factories, GM is certainly fighting back. And so is Chrysler, under the irrepressible leadership of Lee Iacocca. With its recent acquisition of the American Motors Corporation, along with the valuable Jeep nameplate, Chrysler has strengthened its market share and served notice that it intends to keep its Big Three membership.

Ford's foreign competitors, likewise, are responding vigorously by developing new products and even new nameplates and channels of distribution. Honda, which is already the fourth largest auto manufacturer in the United States, has introduced its higher-priced Acura line and has done so through a new and exclusive dealer network. Toyota and Nissan are also developing larger, high-performance, luxury cars to be marketed under the names Lexus and Infiniti. These cars will be introduced to the U.S. market in the 1989-90 models years and will be sold through their own dealer networks to establish a strong brand identity.

The important issue for Ford is whether the process of corporate renewal, which began with the development of the Taurus, has invested the company with those intangible assets of innovativeness and competitive intensity that must be maintained to sustain long-term success. If, as *Popular Science* declared, the introduction of the Taurus "put [Ford] five years ahead of its U.S. competitors," can Ford maintain or even accelerate its momentum so as to keep or, better still, to lengthen that five-year lead? And can the company do so without compromising its newfound commitment to quality?

That commitment is very real and pervasive at Ford. But shortly after the Taurus was introduced, the company learned that creating and maintaining true, comprehensive, and enduring quality in a product as complex as a car is perhaps a harder task than originally thought — especially when that car is so radically different from the norm.

As fresh, exciting, and demonstrably well-built as they were, the first models of the Taurus and Sable gave their owners a variety of problems and the Ford Motor Company some unexpected embarrassment. Only a week after the cars were released, Ford had to recall them to replace a defective ignition switch, and a short time later, some of the cars were recalled to replace improperly tempered window glass. Other problems included an unpleasant odor from the catalytic converter on some of the cars and a minor engine surge caused by a defective microprocessor in the engine's electronic control system.

In addition, the first-year (1986) Taurus tested poorly on government crash tests — a fact that was widely publicized by the media. The 1988 Taurus, however, performed "well" in this category, according to *Consumer Reports* (June 1988). The magazine also pointed out that, according to insurance industry data, fewer than average injury claims have been filed by Taurus drivers.

Another problem noted by *Consumer Reports* is the Taurus's frequency-of-repair record. At least among the readers surveyed by the magazine, that record was unfavorable, although it did improve between the 1986 and 1987 models, and again in 1988. *Business Week* and *The New York Times* quickly picked up on the *Consumer Reports* story and published critical articles about the repair records of the 1986 Taurus and Sable midway through the 1988 model year — or two and a half years after the fact. However, the results of both independent studies and Ford's own surveys show that the frequency-of-repair incidence for the Taurus and Sable has declined by 33 percent since the cars were released on December 26, 1985. Moreover, Allstate and State Farm Mutual have found the *repairability* of the cars after accidents to be so improved that these insurers now give a 30-percent discount to Taurus owners.

Ford's response to the problems the Taurus encountered after its introduction seems to illustrate the company's recognition that quality is not merely a principle to be arbitrarily proclaimed, but a crucial and ongoing strategem for successfully running a business.

The company answers its critics on the quality issue by acknowledging that the 1986 and, to a lesser extent, the 1987 Taurus and Sable have had some problems. But the company points out that virtually all cars have problems upon introduction, and that the Taurus and Sable were "breakthrough" products — among the most all-new cars ever produced in the industry. Ford also offers research evidence showing that 84 percent of Taurus owners are either "completely" or "very" satisfied with their cars.

The company routinely commissions outside research firms to conduct consumer evaluation surveys and durability studies to track what the industry calls "things gone wrong" (TGW). Tests on the first-year Taurus showed the car to be just slightly worse than average in TGW, but similar tests on the 1988 model showed that *no* American car in the same size and price class scored better than Taurus. Testing also shows that the overall quality of all Ford products, as measured by TGW, has improved by 65 percent since 1980. And interestingly, Ford's overall TGW rating is now better than the average for all European cars sold in the United States. It is on the basis of these improving records that the company claims in its advertising that Ford cars and trucks have captured quality leadership among domestic automakers over the past eight years. And while Ford still lags behind the TGW quality levels of some Japanese cars, the company has sliced the Japanese lead in half during this same eight-year period.

The key point is not that the Taurus and Sable had some mechanical troubles in their first year or two, but how Ford has reacted to those troubles. The company never backed off, stuck its head in the sand, or tried to deny that problems existed. And, having embraced new definitions of quality, the company is now fully engaged in pursuing "continuous improvement" — which Donald Petersen declares to be "key in every aspect of our business." It is, according to Petersen, the company's "operating philosophy."

At this point, a fundamental question is: Will the Taurus program and everything it symbolizes for Ford have a long-lasting, favorable impact on the corporation's overall operations and help strengthen the rest of the company's product lines? The prognosis in 1988 seems very good indeed.

Ford's 1988 four-door Lincoln Continental holds great promise in the traditional American luxury-car market. Built on the Taurus platform, the new Continental is a logical extension of the Taurus development experience at Ford. It was designed by a team, with creative and manufacturing-level input from line workers and suppliers, and it was built under Ford's new assembly-line procedures, using methods and advanced technology evolved through the Taurus program. Its pre-release promotion included a Taurus-like caravan tour and a similar ride-and-drive program for dealers and their salespeople. And it was introduced — like the Taurus and Sable—on December 26.

By June 1988, the Continental was sold out for the rest of the year, and customer back-orders were ranging from four to six months, depending upon the geographic region of the country. As with the Taurus and Sable, the Continental received its own rave reviews from the trade press. *Car and Driver* wrote, "The new Continental will change the way the world thinks of the American car." *Auto Week* proclaimed, "This car translates much more of the European standard of luxury into the American idiom. In so doing, it redefines automotive luxury in the U.S. We think it will be a hit."

The Scorpio, built by Ford of Europe and brought to the United States by the Lincoln-Mercury Division, has begun to carve out it own niche in the high-performance "European-style" sports sedan market. Designed to compete head-on against Mercedes, BMW, Audi, Saab, and Volvo, the Scorpio won more awards than any other car when it was introduced in Europe. In 1986, fifty-six automotive journalists representing seventeen countries voted the Scorpio "Car of the Year" in Europe, putting it ahead of such high performers as the Saab 9000 and the Mercedes-Benz 200 and 300E models.

Ford's new Probe, designed by Ford, engineered by Mazda, and assembled in a new plant operated by Mazda at Flat Rock, Michigan, was introduced to the public in May, 1988. By the end of June, dealer back-orders exceeded 100,000 — which represented nearly two-thirds of the plant's 160,000-car-per-year manufacturing capacity. (The Flat Rock plant is designed to produce 240,000 cars per year, but 80,000 of those are Mazda MX6's.) The Probe's target market is one that has been dominated in recent years by the Japanese and Germans: a youthful, better-educated, middle- to upper-middle-income market with a high proportion of females (57 percent). According to consumer studies, the car is perceived by the market as one of the best that the company has ever introduced.

The positioning of the Scorpio and Probe in the U.S. market illustrates the truly global character of Ford's strategy for the 1990s — a strategy which will integrate design, manufacturing, and marketing elements from the United States, Europe, and Japan.

As is the case with the Taurus, the Probe is being exported to Japan, where it is sold through the joint Ford-Mazda "Autorama" dealer network. It is notable that Ford is now the number-one foreign automotive name in the Japanese market, far outpacing all other American and European nameplates. Given the annual six-million-car volume of the Japanese home market, Ford is advantageously postioned there for the future.

In 1989, the Lincoln Continental will also be exported to Japan, along with the newly designed Thunderbird, which is scheduled for release in the American market, once again, on December 26.

Concerning the new Thunderbird, Ray Ablondi says the company is "more than pleased" with consumer reaction to the car from early research studies. Advance specifications for the Thunderbird have already been picked up by the automotive press, and *Auto Week* scored a scoop with photographs of prototypes. Interestingly, the new Thunderbird — which bears a strong resemblance to BMW's top-of-the-line 635 coupe — is a *rear*-wheel-drive vehicle, as are all cars manufactured by BMW, Mercedes-Benz, and Jaguar. In mid-1988, Ford is the only U.S. automaker fully committed to both front-wheel and rear-wheel drive, as GM and Chrysler have turned almost totally to front-wheel. According to Lewis Veraldi, front-wheel drive has proven to be a decided advantage for smaller cars, somewhat of a toss-up for mid-size cars, and something of a disadvantage for larger cars.

Auto analysts point out that Ford, to some extent, "lucked out" on the front-wheel/rear-wheel drive decision, as well as on the question of extreme downsizing. In the 1979–82 period, Ford simply didn't have the money to downsize its entire lineup of cars and convert them all to front-wheel drive. With a few exceptions, however, GM did just that. Then, when the energy crisis abated, Ford was able to capitalize on its position as the dominant domestic producer of larger, more traditionally styled American cars with rear-wheel drive. Those cars included the Lincoln Town Car, the Ford Crown Victoria, and the Mercury Grand Marquis—all of which are built on the same platform and manufactured in the same plant. Originally scheduled to be phased out in 1989, these cars enjoyed such a revival in popularity that they were given a reprieve through 1991. Perhaps the consummate symbols of the classic six-passenger American luxury car — vehicles of almost limousine proportions — the Town Car, the Crown Victoria, and the Grand Marquis continue to attract mature and conservative American drivers, as well as fleet operators such as taxi and limousine companies, funeral directors, and the like.

To be sure, these cars are radically different in concept, style, and proportion from Ford's newer products; but they nonetheless share the company's new and total dedication to quality and customer satisfaction. Year by year during the development of the Taurus and other new cars, Ford's designers and engineers have borrowed ideas, features, and production methods associated with the Taurus, Continental, Probe, and Thunderbird programs. The result has been a steady improvement in the older cars to the point where they have become as dependable and trouble-free as any product in Ford's lineup. In short, since quality became "job one" at Ford, the company's entire assortment of cars, vans, and trucks has shown notable improvements across the board. With the exception of the German-made Merkur XR4Ti, a two-door compact that has had a lackluster sales performance in the United States, the Ford Motor Company did not have a single product introduction from 1985 through 1988 that could be called a failure. Indeed, since the Taurus and Sable hit the streets, Ford has been on a very big roll. The company's worldwide sales for 1987 reached $71.6 billion — a 14 percent increase over the previous year — and from all indications, 1988 will witness similar or superior results.

By contrast, from 1985 through late 1988, General Motors saw its sales and market share drop off significantly in the United States. More ominously, it has been GM's *newer* products that have failed to reach targeted sales levels, and among the biggest disappointments has been the restyled Cadillac line. In the three years from mid-1985 to mid-1988, more than 60,000 Cadillac owners switched to Lincoln alone. The new downsized Eldorados and Sevilles have sold at a much lower rate than the models they replaced, and they have been highly criticized for looking too much like GM's mid-size cars. The compact-sized Cimmaron was actually taken off the market in early 1988 because of poor sales performance. And even the highly publicized Italian-designed

Allante was selling at only about 50 percent of expectations in mid-1988.

Essentially, GM seems to be having trouble deciding what it wants to be in the future. As *Motor Trend* said in February, 1986: "The problem with the [Cadillac] Eldorado stems from a basic GM credo to be everything to everybody ... It's as if Cadillac realizes what it must do, has identified and analyzed its problems, but still can't bring itself to shed the past and get on with the business of rebuilding its reputation as America's most coveted prestige marque."

At the core of the problem may be the lack of a distinct and unified purpose. Ford, during its darkest days of 1979–80, first decided *what* it wanted to achieve, and then called upon a variety of internal and external resources — including the consumer — for ideas about how to reach its goal. But GM in the 1980s may be singlemindedly trying to improve upon certain things that perhaps it shouldn't be doing in the first place.

A 1988 Cadillac sales brochure, for example, touted the car's dazzling features in purple prose: "Electro-luminescent Opera Lamps ... Wreath and Crest Ornamentation ... Diamond Grain II Textured Full Cabriolet Roof Treatments ... Royal Prima Cloth Seating with Contessa Cloth Inserts," and — be still our hearts! — *"Trumpet Horns."*

Does GM know the customer it's speaking to in such turgid language? And does this brochure describe a car that sets a worldwide standard of excellence for luxury-car buyers of today and the coming decade?

In its other forms of advertising, too, GM appeared in 1987 and 1988 to be more or less shouting for attention. The dominant theme of Chevrolet television commercials has been "The heartbeat of America" — an undisguised pitch to patriotism — with Chevrolet, of course, providing the "heartbeat." Brassy and brash, these commercials have typically portrayed an ethnically diverse collection of Americans "doing their thing." Men in hard hats watched well-endowed girls in blue jeans strut past construction sites, families romped with their dogs and kids beside their Chevy van or station wagon, break-dancers cavorted on city streets, and macho guys in cowboy hats congratulated one another for driving a *"today's* Chevrolet." Seldom, however, has there been any real product information in these commercials. Chevrolet vehicles have been displayed in all sorts of settings, but little has been said about them except to claim that they are "America's number-one seller." Even this assertion didn't reflect the current reality. A Chevrolet commercial in late 1987, for example, proclaimed that the Chevy was America's best-selling car "for the last four years combined." Since Ford had actually outsold Chevrolet in 1987, this was the only way GM could lay claim to a "best-selling" car.

Pontiac's 1988 advertising theme has been "We build excitement." Television commercials portray Pontiac owners as a fast-driving, gear-shifting breed, constantly pushing their cars to the limit. The accompanying music is fittingly loud and intense, presumably to emphasize the "excitement." To some viewers, no doubt, these commercials are appealing. But to others they may well smack of recklessness and irresponsibility.

It is the overall contrast between Ford and GM advertising that has been striking. Paradoxically, Ford seems to have assumed GM's traditional role — presenting ads and commercials that are low-key, self-assured, and informative, GM's hyped-up advertising, on the other hand, appears to reflect an anxious mood on the part of the company. Such anxiety is even more apparent in recent GM commercials that are blatantly "Ford-bashing" in character. In one commercial, Ford and Chevrolet trucks are shown standing upright on their tailgates, and the Ford truck eventually crashes to the ground because it ostensibly can't stand up to the "superior" Chevy. In another, a Chevy truck is launched, like a space-shot, while the Ford truck remains rooted to the ground. And in still another, a Ford and Chevy truck "face off" against each other like two angry bulls lowering their heads for a fight — with the Ford truck, of course, giving ground and ultimately falling backwards over a hillside.

Advertising experts may argue that such contentious ads are effective because they command attention and create mental recall. Perhaps so, in some cases. Awareness ratings may indeed be good, and the ads may actually sell more cars in the short run. But will this sort of advertising help to position GM where the company wants to be in the 1990s and beyond? Meanwhile, the question has to be raised: why does Ford continue to recapture domestic market share while GM contines to lose it? Part of the answer undoubtedly is in the product. But while GM struggles to bring its own products up to par, its advertising and promotion strategy doesn't seem to be creating a positive differential.

There is no doubt that GM is still the giant of the domestic industry and that it has formidable resources to bring to battle. But as Ross Perot has said, "The company's problem is not a lack of money but a lack of ideas and priorities." GM has been *company*-focused; Ford has been *customer*-focused. GM has been *internally* oriented and preoccupied with reducing costs; Ford has been *externally* oriented and intent on increasing customer values.

The net result is that GM has become vulnerable at the very heart of its traditional strength — the family mid-market and luxury-car markets. Even its new aerodynamic "Ten" series was released only as two-door coupes, leaving the four-door sedan and station wagon markets wide open to a continuing onslaught by the Taurus, Sable, Scorpio, Continental, and even the big, old Town Car, Crown Victoria, and Grand Marquis. Unfortunately for GM, sales of the 1988 Ten series — the Buick Regal, Oldsmobile Cutlass, and Pontiac Grand Prix — have fallen short of expectations.

In the interest of maintaining a healthy domestic auto industry — an industry that is so vital to the overall American economy — one would hope that GM can soon get back on track. It may well be that the long-awaited Saturn project will provide GM the central focus that the Taurus-Sable program gave to Ford. But even the Saturn project is viewed by many industry analysts with only cautious optimism. For one thing, it has been repeatedly delayed and cut back, and there have even been rumors that it would be scrapped altogether, in spite of the billions of dollars already invested. This sort of vacillation tends to reinforce the idea that the company lacks a coherent sense of purpose and commitment.

By late 1988, there is a growing fear — if not a distinct certainty — that the worldwide auto industry is fast reaching a point of over-capacity: there are too many plants producing too many cars for the market to absorb. GM has finally recognized this, announcing in mid-1988 the permanent closing of several plants and the mothballing of others. In announcing these shutdowns and the resulting worker layoffs, GM officials in effect conceded that the company's market share was not likely to return to its historic levels.

The real issue of the future of America is what role the *entire* U.S. auto industry will play in the evolving worldwide automotive league. Since theearly 1980s, all of the U.S. automakers have bounced back remarkably — with the only exception being the American Motors Corporation, which is now a part of Chrysler. The Big Three collectively reported their highest single-quarter profits ever in the second quarter of 1988. Ford, GM, and Chrysler are solidly in the black, and as noted earlier, Ford's performance makes it the most profitable automotive company in the world.

But the action will increasingly become multinational as U.S. carmakers continue to establish joint ventures with foreign manufacturers and distributors. This trend, which started in the late 1970s and early 1980s, will only intensify as the 1990s unfold. A car might be designed and engineered in one country, its basic components built in one or more others, and its final assembly done in still another. Then the finished vehicle might be loaded onto a ship and transported for sale in any of a dozen other countries. As mentioned earlier, Ford and Mazda are already collaborating on the sale of Ford products in Japan and on the manufacture of the Probe in Flat Rock, Michigan, where Mazda also produces one of its own nameplates. GM's Chevrolet Nova and Toyota's Corolla FX are both manufactured in a California plant. The Pontiac Le Mans, an adaptation of the German-built Opel, is made in Korea. The Ford Motor Company's Mercury Tracer, which bears many similarities to the Mazda 323, is made in

Mexico. And Chrysler's Plymouth Colt, essentially a Mitsubishi, is built in Japan. Furthermore, Ford and Mazda are talking about the possibility of Ford's building small pickup trucks to be sold under the Mazda nameplate in Mazda's own U.S. dealerships. In discussing this potential arrangement, Mazda president Norimasa Furuta described it as "entering an era of true reciprocity." And finally, even China has recently approached both Ford and GM seeking joint ventures to produce American cars in China.

To emerge as such a vigorous competitor in a truly global environment, Ford had to abandon the bankrupt concepts, standards, and methods that had brought the company — and indeed, the whole U.S. car industry — virtually to its knees in the late 1970s. In making its comeback, Ford became a leader not merely by cultivating new attitudes and inventing new rules, but by *integrating* new attitudes and both new and old rules into a workable and profitable whole. Employee involvement, for example, wasn't really a new idea, but Ford made its EI program work in concert with the many other changes that the company undertook as parts of a coherent corporatewide recovery effort. Aerodynamics and ergonomics certainly weren't new ideas either, but if they were to be applied in productive ways, it required employee involvement, better supplier relations, a total dedication to quality, a best-in-class commitment, new assembly line techniques, painstaking research, and extraordinary market conditioning and promotion programs. No single innovation could stand alone and produce the dramatic results that Ford so badly needed. Just as a modern car is a vastly complex piece of machinery that depends upon the coordinated functioning of all its parts, so too is the "machinery" that it takes to build such a car. Change one part, and you'll most likely have to change a number of others. It is this sort of perspective that made Ford the most profitable auto company of all time in 1988. And it's a perspective that more and more American companies are finding they must adopt in order to compete in the global arena of the 1990s.

Philip Caldwells' overall outlook for the U.S. auto industry and for American manufacturing in general is markedly optimistic. Talking with him, one is reassured by his confidence. After all, he's *been* there. Orchestrating the revival of a company that was on the brink of disaster taught Caldwell, Donald Petersen, Red Poling, and many of their 375,000 associates at Ford some crucial lessons that other U.S. business leaders would do well to ponder on their own behalf.

As the nation heads into the 1990s, there is mounting evidence that many U.S. companies, both large and small, are rediscovering the principles that Ford management has delineated so clearly: the importance of *enduring product value* and the *values of people.* Ford learned that there is no substitute for a good product that is addressed to the real needs and wants of the market; and the company learned further that, regardless of title or job description, most people have a remarkable capacity to do the right things in the right way if given the opportunity.

The quality of American products and services is once again on the upswing, and consumers and businesses are once again "buying American," not merely because of union or political sloganeering, but because more American goods and services are *worth* buying.

Things probably never will come full circle again, where the United States is unchallenged as the richest, smartest, and toughest kid on the block. But that may not be a rational objective anyway, because the world is indeed evolving into a global economy in which nations and corporations will enjoy greater mutual benefits through cooperation and friendly competition. The overriding challenge to American business and industry is to become a strong partner in this global economy — by producing better goods and services with more cost-effective methods through the honest collaboration of management, labor, suppliers, government, and consumers.

Like Ford in 1979, America has no choice. But like the Ford commercials say in 1988, American *can* again start "winning the world over."

About the Authors

Alton F. Doody is an internationally recognized consultant who specializes in market positioning and strategic planning for manufacturers, distributors, and retailers. He operates his own firm, the Alton F. Doody Company, based in Petoskey, Michigan.

Mr. Doody, a native of New Orleans, Louisiana, holds a Ph.D. in business administration and served for eleven years as professor of marketing at The Ohio State University, where he won the Outstanding Teacher Award in 1971. He left the academic community to become cofounder of Management Horizons, Inc., a Columbus, Ohio-based management consulting and research company that serves an international clientele.

After leaving Management Horizons, he founded The Doody Company, which worked with major corporations worldwide in designing retailing facilities and developing retail merchandising systems. He sold the Doody Company to devote full time to independent consulting, research, and writing.

Mr. Doody is coauthor, with William R. Davidson, of *Retailing Management*, a college textbook widely used throughout the United States. He is also coauthor, with Stanley J. Shapiro, of *Marketing in America*, and he has written and coauthored many articles for business and professional journals, including the *Harvard Business Review* and the *Journal of Marketing*.

Ron Bingaman, who lives in Columbus, Ohio, is an independent business writer and public relations consultant.

A native of Portsmouth, Ohio, Mr. Bingaman holds a master's degree from The Ohio State University. He is a former reporter and editor for United Press International, and he served for eight years as vice president for corporate affairs at Management Horizons, Inc.

Mr. Bingaman has taught college courses in journalism, business writing, and organizational communications, and he has conducted workshops and seminars on the same subjects for private companies and public agencies. He also served as an administrator at The Ohio State University and as a researcher and editor at Battelle Memorial Institute, one of the world's leading scientific and technological research organizations.

He is coauthor, with Robert Shook, of *Total Commitment*, a book devoted to the career stories of prominent achievers and leaders in American business, science, entertainment, sports, and public life. He was editor of *How to Be the Complete Professional Salesman*, by Robert and Herbert Shook, and he has authored, coauthored, and ghostwritten numerous corporate publications and articles for trade magazines and business journals.

DEC

D

RE

F